ERLUND HUD

A LIFE

First Published 2014

by Peridot Press

12 Deben Mill Business Centre, Old Maltings Approach,
Melton, Woodbridge, Suffolk IP12 1BL

Tel: 01394 389850 Fax: 01394 386893
Email: enquiries@peridot.co.uk
Website: www.peridot.co.uk

ISBN: 978 1 909 717 21 3

Set and designed by Theoria Design
www.theoriadesign.com

Printed and bound in Great Britain
by Cambrian Printers, Aberystwyth

Contents

Introduction and Acknowledgements

Eleanor Hudson died in March 2011 shortly after her 99th birthday. I was subsequently asked by her nieces Virginia Da Costa and Myrth Russell and her nephews Alan Hudson and Hugh Hudson to write the story of their aunt whose life they felt they had never fully known. They had visited her lovely houses but had scarcely been aware, as young adults, of her career as an artist or her involvement in the world of ballet. I am grateful to them for making available to me family papers and for all their help, guidance and hospitality.

I first met Eleanor in 1998 when I was working for the Royal Watercolour Society and saw the name Erlund Hudson (her artistic pseudonym) appear regularly in lists of Honorary Retired Members. Out of curiosity I wrote to her. Although Eleanor had had no contact with the Society since 1960 she replied and invited me to go and see her at her house in Hammersmith Terrace on the bank of the Thames. We sat in her studio and she showed me drawers full of watercolours and sketches which she had scarcely looked at for nearly forty years. I found Eleanor wonderful company, one of the most fascinating people I had ever met. From that first meeting we became friends and our friendship lasted until she died.

Research for this book has been a tremendous pleasure in itself. It has involved travelling north to Argyllshire and as far south as Paris, west to Torquay in Devon where Eleanor was born, and east to the Norfolk coast. However I began in London by talking to Eleanor Garcia, Eleanor's carer and companion for the last years of her life, and I am grateful for her help and suggestions – not least in telling me who I needed to talk to next. I wish also to thank the following: Lazarus Bacchus; Andreas Basler; Jill-Anne Bowden; Peter Bradford; Christine and Lewis Burden; Clare Calder; the late Yvonne Cartier; Magdalen Evans; Betty Eskinazy; Ross Fuller; Patrick Goodison; Roland Goslett; William Griffin; Katherine Hall; Hugh Hamrick; Norman Higgins; Stephen Hudson; Steven and Susanna Levrant; Trata Mahoney; Kim Mendez; Laura Pocock; Prue Seward; Sarah Seymour; Father Julian Shurgold; Andrew Sim; John and Sheila Stenhouse; Father Gideon Wagay; and Ian Whiteman.

I am particularly grateful too to Annette Courtenay-Mayers and Pat Feltham for advice and information on the Gurdjieff Society; and to Anthony Dyson for guidance with regard to printing techniques.

In addition I have been assisted by Hannah Hudson of the Royal Watercolour Society; Mark Pool of Torquay Library; Andrew Potter of the Royal Academy Library; Kari Moodie of Dudley Museums Service; and Patrick Murphy of the Museum of Fine Arts, Boston, Massachusetts.

I also wish to thank my publisher Peridot Press for both their help and patience.

Simon Fenwick, London, April 2014

Preface

I was working in Grays Inn as understudy to my senior law partner when I met Eleanor, who would have been 50 at that time. A working relationship matured to one of trust and friendship.

Simon's book gives insights into Eleanor's sister and four elder brothers and her relations, close and not so close, with them and their families. Her father died when she was eleven and her widowed mother educated them from her income.

In 1934 Eleanor, uninvited, with her drawings arrived at the Royal School of Art seeking admission, which she gained. Later she won a travelling scholarship which she spent in Italy until the outbreak of war.

In 1948 Eleanor's American or more accurately Norwegian-American mother died. Interestingly her mother, a widow living in Devon for many years, never returned to live in the States, her old home and the source of the fortune made by Eleanor's grandfather.

Eleanor was an artist. She had limited interest in world affairs and home in a burgeoning social life. At a Brooking Ballet School meeting Nesta presented apologies for absence adding, and these words could easily have come from Eleanor, the explanation that she had gone to wherever it was that people went in late June.

When Eleanor was a few years short of 40 she received her share of her grandfather's fortune and her share of her mother's property. Eleanor's aim was to help others in small or not so small ways. Her London home became 6 Hammersmith Terrace and later she bought at auction the site on the Trippet at Bosham, where with her architect friend she built her dream home, which she and her friends enjoyed almost to the end of her days.

Eleanor kept these homes for 50 years or longer. She died in Camden Street, Nesta's home, which she bought from her.

Christopher Wright

Chapter One – St Marychurch

Eleanor Hudson lived most of her life close to the water's edge. The sea or the bank of the river was just a short walk or a bike ride away, or at the bottom of her garden

Eleanor Erlund Hudson was born on the 18th of February 1912 in a house called Weston in St Marychurch on the outskirts of Torquay in Devon. She did not begin to call herself 'Erlund Hudson' until she was in her twenties and had started to exhibit as an artist but to her family and friends she was always known as Eleanor. From Massachusetts her parents received congratulations from Nellie Blood, her grandmother's former secretary: 'At last the cable has come and brought us the glad tidings that you have a little daughter and that all was well!' After a succession of five brothers, the youngest of whom had died only a few months earlier, Eleanor was a welcome second daughter to Harold Hudson and his wife Helen. Unlike some of her elder brothers, she was a healthy baby, but over the years the problem of her health was to be a constant in her own story, and she grew up surrounded by family conversations about her own strength and by the various sicknesses of her father and her brothers. Eleanor was also born into a country where there was fear of war with Germany,

Harold Hudson

Helen Hudson

demands for Home Rule for Ireland, strikes and suffragettes (in another of her letters Nellie said she thought the suffragettes were worse than the strikers because they threw stones and smashed windows). Many feared their world was falling apart. Then in April a few weeks after Eleanor's birth the Titanic sank.

It was remarkable that Eleanor's parents should ever have met at all. Harold was the son of a surgeon who had run a hydropathic clinic in the Lake District. He worked in Liverpool in the export trade but severe rheumatic pain forced Harold to retire and in 1898 he set out to travel around the Mediterranean in search of relief and a cure. At the beginning of December 1899 he arrived in Menton on the Riviera which at the time was not so much a resort as a colony for the sick. A Scottish doctor had declared the town ideal for patients suffering from lung problems – which it was not – and its numerous villas and hotels filled with ailing guests gave Menton a peculiarly depressing atmosphere. Harold had booked to stay at the Belle-Vue Hotel which was supposedly the best hotel in town. He was 41, a short man and slightly built with a high forehead, blue eyes, brown hair and a red moustache, and temperamentally rather dry and unsentimental.

Helen's background was very different. She came from a large family network of intermarrying Norwegian-American emigré cousins. Her father Peder Olsen left Norway in 1852 when he was sixteen and penniless but by hard work and study he had become Treasurer of the Bliss Fabyan Corporation, the largest cotton goods manufacturer in the world, and a leading industrialist in Boston, Massachusetts. In 1861 he had married his cousin Ingeborg Anderson but as she had grown older osteo-arthritis had made her a bed-ridden invalid. They had three daughters, Anna, Grace and Helen. Anna was already married but her sisters Grace, who was sickly, and Helen still lived with their parents in their large Scandinavian-style mansion in Brookline on the outskirts of Boston. Their father thought that his two younger daughters should go to Europe in order to gain some culture. They were to be accompanied by their mother's cousin, Rebecca Erlund, 'Aunt Becca', as chaperone. 'Aunt Becca' was very much part of the family. Before her marriage Ingeborg had been engaged to Becca's elder brother,

Carl, but he died when he was young. Eleanor and all her family always saw their Norwegian-American roots as part of their identity.

Becca, Helen and Grace sailed from New York to Europe on the SS Augusta-Victoria and arrived at the Belle-Vue Hotel in Menton on November 30th 1899 on the day before Harold. Helen was 27. She was pretty with large, bright eyes and soft, wavy hair with a plait tied up in a bun. She was also a determined young woman who knew her own mind. For Harold it was love at first sight. Years later, in an untypical moment, he reminisced: 'One day, sitting in the hotel lounge in my bath chair, I looked up and saw a very beautiful young American lady come into the lounge.' Both he and Grace looked for sheltered places in which to sit and, as Helen joined her ailing sister, she and Harold were often in one another's company. They also went for walks together. As they grew to know one another better so Harold's health, according to family legend, improved rapidly and he felt able to abandon his cure. 'It just *grew*,' Helen said of her relationship. On February 15th 1900, less than three months after she met Harold, she wrote home to Ingeborg:

> My own dearest Mamma
>
> In one of your recent letters you asked me to write and tell you what I had been doing and thinking, but I'm afraid you never dreamt what I would answer, and you must be a good, dear lady and please be very indulgent to your "baby" when she "fesses". For it's a big confession this baby has to make to you and to Papa, and one which will trouble and surprise you very much, yet is one which has come to pass and "come to stay", that your minor child (that was) has been and gone and fallen in love with the very dearest Englishman in the world - indeed he is, Englishman or no Englishman - the very dearest man in all the world except my own Papa who can never be equalled but you see as I have him for a father I don't need him for a husband, and I do need Harold Hudson very badly.

She was set on marrying him, pointing out that England was only five days sail from America whereas 'California or Seattle or some such place... would be ever so much worse'. Even better, 'he himself is more like an American than any Englishman I've ever met, with a very keen sense of humor and a bright way of looking at things'.

Aunt Becca reassured Helen's parents that Harold was acceptable and by April he and Helen were engaged. Harold himself would have been unable to provide for his new wife in a way to which she had become accustomed and, whatever Peder Olsen thought of his son-in-law, he drew up a marriage settlement which ensured that his daughter kept control of her own money. In August 1900 Harold and Helen were married in Brookline. Ingeborg was brought early to the church, lifted from her carriage, and placed behind a screen so that the congregation could not see her but she was able to follow the service. A few weeks later the newly married couple sailed to Sorrento, only returning to America in July the following year when they settled in Pinehurst in North Carolina. In a tiny red diary in an entry for March 13th 1902 Harold wrote that he had enjoyed a good game of golf, then at the very bottom of the page, he squeezed in, 'Elizabeth was born'. In September, Harold, Helen and their new baby all sailed back across the Atlantic, and stayed at the Grand Hotel de Nice in San Remo for six months. They finally arrived in England in March 1903 and in May their eldest son, Edmund Peder, was born at Temple Cowley outside Oxford.

Peder Olsen

In August the following year Harold and Helen at last found somewhere permanent to settle, finding their future home in St Marychurch, an old village which had been absorbed into the northern edge of Torquay. Harold had relations in south Devon so it is possible that he may already have known the area. The 1910 *Baedeker* guide described Torquay as:

> a town of modern growth, with 33,625 inhab., beautifully situated on the N.W. angle of ***Tor Bay***, [it] is a favourite resort of persons with delicate chests, on account of its mild and equable climate; and it contests with Brighton and Scarborough the title of Queen of English watering - places. In winter the thermometer seldom descends to 36° Fahr., while in summer the maximum heat is about 77°. The town, seen to greatest advantage from a boat in the bay, is spread over a number of small hills, which rise in terraces above the sea, and are dotted with well-built villas embosomed in a luxuriant semi-typical vegetation scarcely paralleled elsewhere in England. "It reminds one of Newport", says an American writer, "in the luxuriousness of its foliage, the elasticity of its lawns, and its masses of flowers". The bathing and boating are excellent, and the environs abound in charming walks and drives. Torquay is an important yachting station, and an annual regatta is held in Aug. or Sept., while packs of harriers and fox-hounds are within easy reach. Golf is played at Babbacombe Down.

It must have seemed ideal.

Number 26 Church Street – Weston – was one of a row of houses clustered around the large medieval parish church which gave St Marychurch its name. This was the church the Hudson family attended, and where two of Eleanor's brothers played the organ and sang in the choir with the village boys who wore patched clothes under their cassocks. Nearby there was a pub called the Cary Castle and a large Roman Catholic church. Fore Street, a long, narrow street lined with shops, ran downhill into Babbacombe while other roads and paths led into fields, back to Torquay, or down the cliffs to Oddicombe Beach on the edge of Babbacombe Bay. Weston itself was a substantial Victorian villa built in the 1860s. The house had always been called Weston although by chance 'Weston' was also the name of the village in Massachusetts where Helen's sister Grace lived after her own marriage. The kitchens, the basement and the servants' quarters as well as the garage for Harold's much-loved car and the sheds for garden equipment all faced onto Church Street which made the house seem the wrong way round. The dark-panelled main rooms looked out over the garden where the extensive lawns were used for tennis and croquet, and beyond the kitchen garden was full of fruit trees and vegetable beds. At the time of Eleanor's birth there was an indoors staff of four: a nursemaid, a cook, a parlour-maid, and a second maid in the nursery. There was also a gardener and handyman called Joseph Padden who worked at Weston for many years. Much later in life Eleanor commented on how difficult it had become to find staff to live in: it was what she was used to. There was always a certain accepted standard of living, and the silver tableware – the soup tureens, vegetable dishes, gravy boats dutifully polished by the maids – was always used for Sunday and Christmas lunch.

Weston

Eleanor

After Elizabeth and Edmund, four more boys were born in succession: Harold Paige in March 1905; Laurence Whitmarsh in June 1906; Merivale Lord in July 1908; and Anders Roy in September 1910 (the four eldest children were all christened in America). The younger brothers became increasingly sickly. Laurence suffered from bouts of pneumonia and Merivale was weak and small. Harold believed that there were problems with the Weston drains and when Anders died at only six months he insisted the council dig up the drains and rebuild them. Before long Helen was pregnant again and Eleanor was born only five months after the death of Anders. Eleanor's second name emphasised her Norwegian heritage. There were several Erlunds on Helen's side. Helen spoke Norwegian as a second language, and in time she had a Norwegian daughter-in-law to whom she could speak Norwegian. And it was also by her distinctive, Norwegian, second name that her daughter, Eleanor Erlund Hudson later chose to be known by the art world.

When the First World War broke out Harold joined the Home Guard. For several months from December 1915, when Eleanor was almost three, he was billeted at Mullion on the Lizard Peninsula in the far west of Cornwall in order to guard the remote Poldhu Wireless Station, the station from where in 1901 Marconi had made the first ever Trans-Atlantic wireless signals. Helen and he sent frequent letters to one another and the children travelled by Newton Abbott via Truro to Helston to stay with him for short periods. They exchanged news about the children and about their own lives separated from one another, and Harold also wrote a little about his work:

> A body came up into Poldhu beach last night & it was on the shore all morning covered with a tarpaulin. Most of our men went down and inspected it. They say it was a young man, dreadfully damaged and he had nothing left on but his boots. This with the body at Gunwalloe & another reported at Mullion Cove makes three which have been washed up. I have kept things dark from the children.

It was a close, loving family with anxious parents, a strict, Victorian father and a more indulgent mother. On the same day Helen wrote back:

> Paige is in bed with a cold but it's practically well now. Merivale rode out on the pony this afternoon and Edmund had a fine game of hockey coming back very brisk this afternoon & pleased with things. He seemed like a lost chord without Elizabeth and Paige and has amused himself with The Bluebells of Scotland, which has emanated from the dining room at all sorts of odd hours... Eleanor is deep in "The Army" the book I gave Edmund full of pictures of soldiers, guns & things. She likes it better than Mother Goose.

The following Sunday they all went to church – despite Helen's absence of teeth following a recent visit to the dentist – for a service of intercession. 'I thought of you all through and I wished you were there... everybody felt it all intensely. I saw handkerchiefs all over the church as well as my own,' she wrote.

On December 30 the SS Persia was sunk in the Mediterranean south of Crete by a German U-boat. It was the first passenger ship in WWI to be sunk without warning. 'Those bloody Huns must still be feeling confident or else they would hardly continue sinking passenger ships and murdering helpless civilians,' fulminated Harold. It brought matters closer to home. Among the hundreds of dead and missing was the husband of someone they knew, and Helen wrote of her own personal anxieties:

> The thought of Mary Wrey kept going on in my mind too for they think the first report [that he had been rescued] was not true & now they can't find any trace or get any news and she has gone to London in case of being able to investigate any reports but all things point to the fear that her husband has been lost. Only one more of many thousands of wives left alone for good & all but the thought of being always alone and having to go on living and "carrying on" is so awful, I don't know how it would be possible to carry the burden and not faint and fail.

Eleanor, who despite being nearly three was still known as 'Baby' begins to make her presence felt. Helen describes Paige's return from Mullion on 11 January:

> Perhaps you can imagine the enthusiasm at the meeting, Paige, Laurence & Baby all shouting & jumping up & down at once. I heard Paige describing at great length a pudding with yellow layers & bananas & other glories.

And in a letter written the following day we hear, briefly, Eleanor's own voice:

> Dearie, Baby wants to write a letter to Father. Dear Father Dear (all the family enumerated) did go to Mullion and dear Mother writing a letter. Dear Baby says her prayers at night and doesn't suck her thumb. Dear people come and have a party and Baby woke up Ida [the nursemaid]. Miss Robertson she's coming to my house sometime and see Baby in bed. Dear Hetty takes the dinner in the dining room & the breakfast in the dining room. Father is to Mullion and Paige come back from Mullion. Dear Mother is ***werry well***; once she didn't have any breakfast. And say dear Father and dear Father twice. (Ida calls and off flies the correspondent.)

Eleanor could always tell a story.

Harold was a strict, rather distant, and typically Victorian figure. He was the man who used to come into Eleanor's small bedroom in the morning to wet shave behind a screen. He liked and expected promptness in everyone, including the maid who had to bring him coffee in his study at precisely 11.00 every morning. Corporal punishment was used to instil punctuality as well as for misdemeanour. He wrote to Helen:

> I think you make a mistake to tell Laurence to practise [the piano] after tea. It is better to have a stated time... At 6 he is bound to hear the clock & you also. Then if the clock finishes striking before he starts, cane him well each and every night it happens.

Eleanor's early memories of her brothers were of 'an enchantingly interesting rough and tumble in the house and garden of four creatures known to me and to my brother and big sister as 'the BOYS''.[1] Elizabeth was given the thankless task by her father to instil into them their 'spontaneous pleasures into something known as good behaviour'. Her success was limited – a neighbour once witnessed the sight of her vain attempts at control when all four boys decided that the way to descend from the tram in Market Street was via the outside of the front end rather than the staircase at the back.

Eleanor felt closest to her brother Merivale who was only four years older than her. He was not bookish but he was happy at home and outdoors wandering round the garden with his father who was not generally given to playing with his children. Merivale was rather small from childhood – Eleanor said that he reminded her of Pooh Bear – and Harold called him his 'Little Button'. The three elder sons had grown tall and Harold wondered if the Doctor should be asked about Mémé's [Merivale's] appearance. Perhaps there was something stuck in the back of his throat which prevented him from getting proper nourishment and growing? As a result of his general weakness Merivale's small misdemeanours were tolerated far more than those of his brothers who suffered regular beatings. One Christmas however he lied about some lost keys, an offence considered so unforgiveable that as a punishment he was forbidden by his father to hang up his Christmas stocking. In his distress he crept into a cupboard to cry. Eleanor, who was about six, squeezed in after him and let Merivale weep on her shoulder. She told him she would marry him.

Edmund and Paige were educated at Marlborough College in Wiltshire where they both thrived in the school's sporting and academic atmosphere. Because of his health Laurence half-boarded: he went to school in Newton Abbott during the week and came home at the weekends. He loved books and poetry and, as Eleanor put it, 'diverse occupations such as the taking-to-pieces with ease the workings of household clocks – and the non-solutions of putting them together – to the chagrin of the home.'[2] Merivale followed Edmund and Paige to Marlborough but his time in the school was much less successful – he was not in any way academic, just 'adequate', a fact which his teachers cruelly pointed out – and he could not compete with his older brothers' outstanding careers. Eventually he was taken out of school and sent to a distant cousin of Helen in Arizona. Here he had his own horse and spent eighteen months with other horsemen and when at last he came back Merivale was a different man, both physically and mentally.

As she grew older Eleanor too was frequently ill, her poor health being blamed on the fact that she was born during Helen's menopause. Her first school was St Winifred's in Abbey Road in Torquay but she was frequently absent. While romping with some big children in a field she fell face down onto the ground and a bigger, thirteen-year old girl jumped onto her spine. Although she was hurt she managed to stand up but two or three days later she could not get out of bed and she began to miss so much school work that the school wrote and asked for her to be withdrawn. A weak heart was diagnosed and the doctors said she must rest. In all Eleanor spent about a year in bed. Like many children she loved to draw and so, encouraged by her mother, she passed the hours sitting in bed drawing and over time her very real talent began to develop. 'Eleanor will be an artist,' everyone said, and Eleanor herself believed this too. But the year in bed also determined the course of her life in another way. Because she was encouraged to rest and lacked exercise for so long a time she did not develop physically as she should have done; her back was never strong and throughout her life it caused her great, and eventually disabling, pain. Although she received help in later years with the help of an osteopath she had already abused her back by thinking she could do too much. All this was to play a significant part of her future.

Asked what she remembered of her father, Eleanor said simply that Harold was 'always ill'. In the summer of 1923 Elizabeth and Laurence accompanied him to Harrogate where he went for treatment but in October, shortly after his return, he died of emphysema. He was 65. He was buried in the far corner of the cemetery at Barton, close to the boundary wall, where the afternoon sun catches the gravestone. Edmund, who was studying Natural Sciences at King's

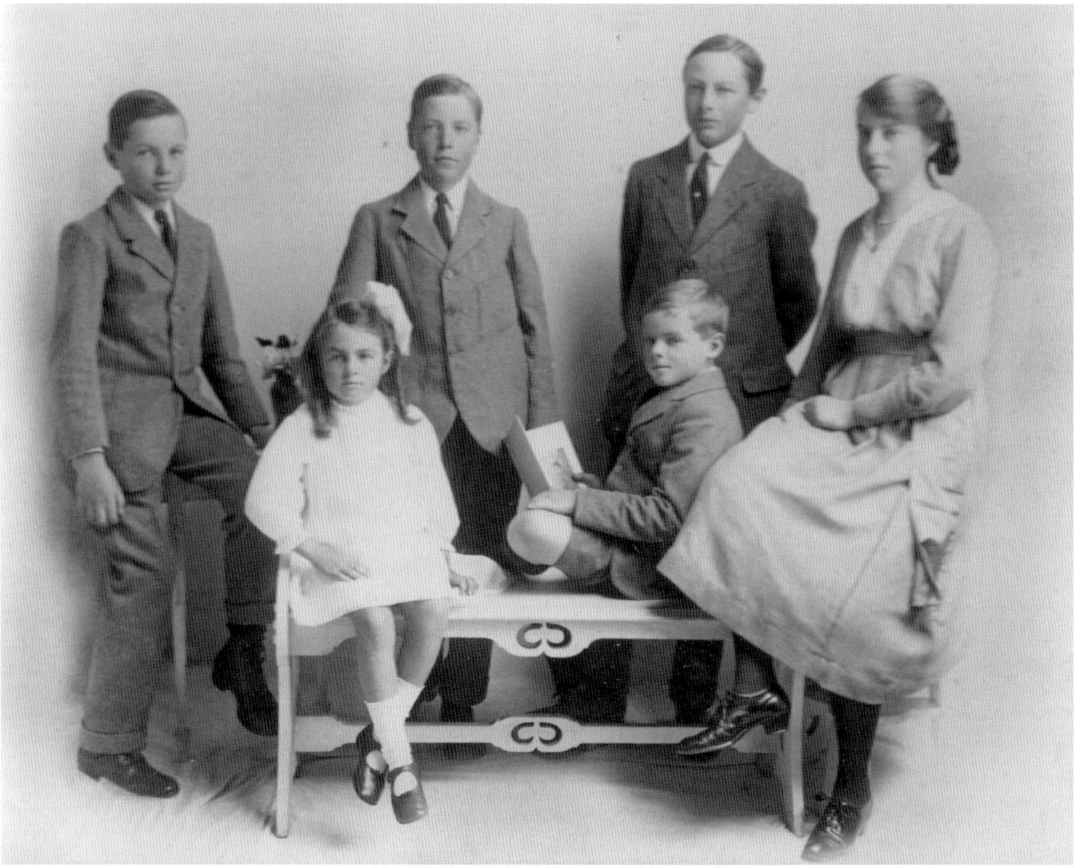

Laurence, Eleanor, Paige, Merivale, Edmund, Elizabeth

College, Cambridge, took on many of the family's responsibilities. The following year he sailed to America to see the trustees of the estate of Peder Olsen (who had died sixteen years earlier) in order to secure the family's future financial arrangements. In September Helen wrote to him about the arrangements for his return. The letter was also much concerned about domestic matters ('I have got one eye on the Linoleum man in the other room and with another one on you or the landing stage, so to speak'), Beatrice the cook (who 'is to go as she is getting quite impossible') and the carpenters who were putting asbestos in the attic. She also wrote about her worries:

> The various illnesses take it out of one, and Eleanor is a weight on my heart, as it is so sad that she cannot be well and strong, everything about her being so well and healthy. I had a heart-to-heart talk with Dr. Catford yesterday about her and he

> is inclined to think she should not go to school this winter. He says everything is a question of what amount of strain the heart will stand - i.e. it is all a matter of what will be over-strain and it may take a long time before quite ordinary things will not be too much tax on the heart. He considers that that was what happened in that Sunday afternoon walk; although she seemed so well, she was not well enough for the heart to do that amount. So one can only give her rest and as much fresh air as possible and sun, and feel one's way for the rest. She was to sit up for a little while, not dressed, yesterday and slowly increase till he comes again on Tuesday.[3]

All in all Eleanor had very little formal education. Her doctors were of the opinion that she could not cope with the pressure of attending a normal school where she would be expected to sit examinations. Instead she was sent for a couple of years to a boarding school in Dorking in Surrey which was more like a finishing school than an ordinary school and there were a lot of foreign girls taking English classes. Pupils received a proper music education but art classes were particularly uninspiring, mere pencil exercises in still-life drawing: a jug, a bar of soap, a step-ladder. Although the girls were taken up to London to visit the galleries everything else was old-fashioned and completely lacking in stimulation. And then at the end of term she recalled how she used sit with her nose pressed against the train windows as she travelled across country looking out for the sea-breakers and the cliffs of the south Devon coast on her journey home.

In 1925 on her thirteenth birthday Edmund wrote to Eleanor from King's:

> I hope that you have a very pleasant holiday and lots of nice presents. Only, you must not grow too fast, just because you are thirteen. And you will have to be careful all through the year, not to break mirrors or to walk under ladders, etc, because 13 is an unlucky number; it is mine. The unluckiest people in the world were those born on Friday, the 13th day of the 13th month of 1313, that is, on Friday, Decembruary 13th, 1313. They put in an extra month then, especially for the benefit of these people.
> I suppose you have been hard at work at school, learning all about Geography and Geometry, and that various colds have quite mended. I wonder if you've been playing any games or going for any walks in crocodiles. The other day, when I got up, I smelt Spring for the first time this year. Have you smelt her yet? There are hundreds of crocuses racing up above the grass near my rooms, and the buds on one tree just outside my window are growing fast. And I saw some almond blossom the other day. It will soon be summer. I don't like winter. But if some summer comes soon, then winter follows and you will be 14. Don't be 14. Stay young; stay 13 always.
>
> Much love
> Edmund[4]

Eleanor, Helen and Paige

So far Eleanor had no ideas other than to be an artist but at the end of her school years when she returned home to look after Helen, who was unwell, she felt dispirited and wondered if a career in art was going to be a realistic possibility after all.

By 1928 Merivale was studying at Sidney Sussex College, Cambridge and enjoying a succession of girlfriends. Eleanor made sure that she attended the summer ball. She was 16, still young for her age and rather plump. She wore round-framed spectacles, her hair was short and parted down the middle. Not long afterwards her sister Elizabeth married Raymond Ashley, a widower whom she had met when visiting relations in America. His late wife Hilda had been Elizabeth's cousin. She had died in childbirth leaving three young boys. Ray Ashley was a businessman, friendly, sporty and open, always ready with a joke. (His brother Clifford Ashley was a recognised marine artist and had also written the standard book on knots.) To everyone he seemed like a typical American whereas Elizabeth although good-humoured was rather bossy. She returned often to England but began to speak with a strong American accent.

Paige made a cine film of the wedding party gathered on the front lawn at Weston. In the jerky black and white film the men stand around smoking and laughing. Ray plays a mouth-organ and another man, despite wearing morning dress, does a cartwheel over the grass. The women do not smoke but they sit together and chat. They all wear preposterous hats. Violet Hindle Baker, a cousin on the Hudson side and famous in the family for her wonderful stories, is as tall and thin and angular as a crane and she stands in her furs and long beads. Eleanor appears from time to time cheerful and smiling. In another shot Padden the gardener comes into sight, as if indifferent to everything, and walks in front of the conservatory. Paige – who loved ships as well as cine cameras – also filmed the wedding party as they gathered together a few days later at Southampton docks, and the Americans made ready to sail on the SS Pennland of the Red Star Line. They watch as Ray's car hovers overhead before being lowered onto the ship.

Helen had invested her money in land and property and in her widowhood she developed these interests, particularly in planning and building developments. She became an active – and no doubt formidable – figure in both the St Marychurch Traders' Association and the National Playing Fields Association. She had a long controversy with Torquay Town Council regarding the acquisition of some of her land for use as a housing estate which finally had to be bought from her by compulsory purchase. Another of her hobbies was architecture and she renovated and restyled several small properties. Her plans for Barton Parsonage were largely adopted; the first woman to enter the completed parsonage was said to have commented on 'the obvious feminine influence in design'[5]. It was also well known that she was prepared to spend an inordinate amount of time and money writing letters trying to get back paltry amounts – as little as a penny – which she felt she had been overcharged. But her children always adored her.

Helen suggested that Eleanor go for lessons at the Torquay School of Arts and Crafts which, for £3 a term, offered courses in architecture, design, drawing, painting or crafts. The School was in a small, red brick, chapel-like building which had been given to the town by a local philanthropist at the end of the previous century. The activities took place in one very large studio. In one part of the room a group of old ladies sat painting flowers and around the stove another group were drawing a life model who posed respectably clad in a bathing suit. Eleanor's early drawings were remarkably strong and confident. They showed that despite a lack of training she was a natural draughtsman and could hold a line confidently. Of even more interest to Eleanor was another little group who worked in the kitchen where an enthusiastic teacher called Mr Pollard encouraged her to etch on copper plates with acid. The more she worked, the more her belief returned that she must be an artist.

1 EEH to Hugh Hudson, September 2001

2 Ibid

3 Helen Hudson to Edmund Hudson, 11 September 1925

4 Edmund to EEH, 17 February 1925

5 Obituary of Helen Hudson, Torquay Times, 22 October 1948

Chapter Two – The Royal College of Art

Eleanor, 1930s

In 1934, the year she went to the Royal College of Art, Eleanor was twenty-two, lively and confident. She no longer wore her owl-like spectacles and she had pinned her hair up at the back of her head in a French pleat; with her bright eyes and beautiful bone structure she was very attractive indeed. She dressed well: all her life Eleanor was interested in clothes both for herself and as a subject for her work, and, having been trained by a professional needle-woman, she was an excellent needle-woman herself. Her sister and her brothers were making their way in the world, and she had every reason to believe that she would too.

After graduation Edmund continued post-graduate research at the Cavendish Laboratory in Cambridge under the Nobel prize-winner Sir Ernest Rutherford. However, feeling that he had no bent for an academic career, he instead joined Imperial Chemical Industries (ICI) at Billingham on Teesside. In 1934 he married Bodil Böschen, the sister-in-law of a Norwegian cousin. They had met when she was staying at Weston with Helen to learn English. Eleanor was a bridesmaid at the wedding in Norway. Paige, on leaving New College, Oxford, went on a world tour. Laurence, Eleanor and he had all been given an excellent music education, and because he could not bear to live without music he took his wind-up gramophone and his records with him. After his return Paige took a job at Milner Court, the Junior King's School, Canterbury, which was work he loved. In 1933 he married a teacher, Susan Stanley, whom he had met on a teaching course. Eleanor said that Laurence was their mother's favourite son because he looked so much like Peder Olsen, her own father. He was always regarded as very good-looking, the best-looking of the brothers. Like Paige he went to New College, Oxford, and subsequently he studied at the Royal College of Music and the Royal College of Organists. Laurence's whole life revolved around music. (Eleanor, Helen and he once encountered Edward Elgar in a lift in The Green Dragon Hotel in Hereford during the Three Choirs Festival.) Eleanor recalled how one summer she stayed with her brother when he was teaching at Radley College: 'I valued the impromptu music-making after school concerts on into the summer nights from within a lamp-lit cottage where he lodged – say of some famous string trio who couldn't stop from playing – with the companionship of a rapt audience sitting [outside].'[1] In 1937 Laurence married Linda Tabberer, whom he met in St Marychurch and at the Royal College of Music where she was also a student.

Merivale, the youngest brother, went to work on a farm in Norfolk with a friend of Edmund. High-spirited and warm-hearted but somewhat tactless, he phoned his family to tell them to look in the next day's Forthcoming Marriages column in *The Times*. There they learnt that he was engaged to a girl called Joan Bullen so they all went up to Norfolk to inspect her. Norfolk appeared to be much more sophisticated than Devon for here girls were wearing lipstick, smoking, and drinking in pubs. Helen was quite mystified by such racy behaviour. However Joan's background was deeply unfortunate. The family had lost all their money and their jewellery business in Norwich during the financial crash of the 1930s, her father had died and an uncle had committed suicide. Merivale very much wanted to save them from their past. With financial assistance from his mother and brothers he bought an apple farm and a house for his new wife at Hoveton St Peter on the Broads and before long Joan and he had a baby daughter. The Hudsons looked forward to a return on their investment.

The Hudsons knew nothing about the world of art nor did they know any artists who might have been able to help Eleanor further her career so she had to act on her own initiative. At the beginning of the autumn term of 1934 Eleanor travelled up to London with a portfolio of her work and a list of art schools which taught print-making. First on her list was the Royal College of Art, one of the oldest and most prestigious art colleges. Its Principal was Sir William Rothenstein, both an eminent painter in his own right and a highly influential and well-connected figure on the contemporary British art scene. According to the proper process of applying for the print-making course the candidate had to submit six 'careful' drawings of figures, landscape or architecture, and sit an entrance examination consisting of a line drawing of a draped or nude figure and a drawing from life in chalk or pencil. Instead Eleanor walked into the college with her portfolio under her arm and asked for the secretary. A uniformed official sent her to see Athol Hay the registrar and she said could she have a place, please. Hay replied that this was all a bit out of order but he sent her along to see Sir William. When Eleanor opened up her portfolio of paintings, sketches and etchings to show Rothenstein, he was nonplussed to see figures of girls in bathing costumes, and he wondered why there were no nudes. Eleanor was rather shocked by this and told him 'because it wouldn't be decent', and her art school did not do that sort of thing. Nevertheless Rothenstein said that she had 'quite an idea' and told her that there was an empty stool in the School of Engraving, someone else having dropped out. Eleanor took her place in the School and found digs in The Boltons in South Kensington.

The Royal College of Art was then still part of the Victoria and Albert Museum. The Engraving School was in a long gallery with ten windows at each of which stood two work ta-

Jane Boulanger and Newspaper
Etching

H/c printer's proof

Nude study
graphite on buff paper

bles where students sat working on copper plates in shaded daylight. The gallery ended in a staircase which went down into the Museum's Print Room so the students could go down and study the works of the great print-makers of the past. Another flight of stairs went up from the gallery to the work rooms and the printing press. There were two Professors: Malcolm Osborne and Robert Austin. Osborne had been head of the school since 1924 and he specialised in landscapes and portraiture. Eleanor found him pleasant but uninspiring. Austin was only five years younger than Osborne but he was far more dynamic.

Print-making was regarded as both a fashionable and important artistic medium. The Print Revival in England began with James MacNeill Whistler and his brother-in-law Seymour Haden. In 1880 Haden founded a society for print-makers which became the Royal Society of Painter-Etchers and Engravers, the word 'Painter' implying that the print-making was being used as a creative, rather than just a reproductive medium. This revival was at its height in the 1920s. An etching or engraving was seen as much an expression of the artist's ability and feeling as any drawing and the process of inking and wiping of the plate appreciated as capable of making each impression subtly unique. Robert Austin was a significant artist in his own right. The son of a Leicester cabinet-maker and a former student of the RCA, he was an outstanding natural draughtsman who made his reputation as a print-maker during the decade with a series of line-engravings. These engravings were works of great precision and purity which were made with a 'burin'[2], a traditional tool which had been used since the time of Dürer and, with consummate skill, by reproductive engravers of later times. Scarcely anyone was doing prints of

Robert Austin
graphite

this kind and they sold for very high prices. His engravings were first published in 1920 by Molly Bernhard-Smith, the owner of the XXI Gallery in London, who had also given some of the first shows of artists such as Jacob Epstein, Graham Sutherland, Henri Gaudier-Brzeska, and Walter Sickert. Following the financial crash of 1929 the bottom dropped out of the print market but Austin went on to do some of his finest work in the 1930s by which time he had returned to teach at the Royal College.

Austin taught each of the basic techniques of printing which an artist might use. However all of Eleanor's works were intaglio prints – either etchings or, more rarely, dry points. Intaglios differ from relief or lithographic prints in that the ink is held in the crevices of the plate rather than on the surface. A skilled printer applies the ink with a 'dabber' charging the grooves and pits of the plate then uses the palm of his hand to wipe off and create fine variations of tone. In an etching the line is as sharp or blunt as the 'needle' the artist requires, the needle being the instrument used to expose the metal through an acid-resistant ground.[3] In a dry-point the line is scratched and distressed so that the ink is trapped around the edges of the grooves as well as within them. Along with print-making Austin taught life-drawing at a time when it was still regarded as almost a moral virtue as well as central to the training of artists and the measure of a student's progress. For all that such repetition was tiresome it provided the skills that a painter, sculptor or illustrator would need to earn his or her living. Austin held his classes in a small room – a former corridor – into which he placed the easels and an old sofa on which the model posed. He crowded as many students as he could into the space so that the intimacy forced them to see how closeness makes people appear distorted in the real world. Drawing became a way of exploring the problems of reality. Austin enjoyed challenging his students further by posing his models in unexpected positions and then having the models keep the same pose for a whole day. In his keenness to stress a point he would even prod a model's body in order to demonstrate under-lying bone structure. Once a fortnight students' pictures were pinned up in class and discussed. Eleanor said she learnt much from him and that he undid what was misguided in her drawing. Her work shares Austin's accuracy of observation and the same ability to keep her line as she drew. She made the models she sketched in class seem to be people with character and feeling and not just an exercise or an arrangement of flexible shapes. Although the finished work was often very different Eleanor adopted Austin's ideas. A figure kneeling in prayer in an Austin engraving re-appears in her work as a woman kneeling on the floor sewing. But most of all what she shared with him was her intense fascination with people: like Austin she thought humanity the true subject matter of art.

Eleanor's closest friend at the College was Ruth Aspden from Blackburn in Lancashire; she was three years older than Eleanor and had already studied for six years at Blackburn School of Art. They shared a table together in the Engraving School. Ruth was slim and bespectacled like an academic, slightly taller than Eleanor, and with her dark hair in the same fashionable French pleat. The two girls were temperamental opposites. Whereas Eleanor was lively and outgoing, Ruth was quieter, thoughtful and dependable. They became inseparable and went everywhere together. Ruth called Eleanor 'Cherub' and Eleanor invented an endearment for her friend, 'Darlingen'. Ruth and other friends were invited down to Weston where they were introduced to the Hudson family.

London life at the Royal College of Art away from home was a new and liberating experience. In a letter to Eleanor, Ruth describes how comfortable students were about posing for one another:

Robert Austin, Eleanor wearing a hat
graphite

> B. and E. have just gone. We worked hard this evening. A. arrived at a quarter to six. I had not been back more than about 10 - 15 minutes from taking the parcel of drypoint plates to the post office, and was in the throes of washing up... We started work quite soon - in my room (yours looked so terribly unlived in and not at its best in daylight). A. liked the light but I'm afraid it erred in the other direction and was very full of stuff. I had meant to do quite a bit of clearing up before they came but alas!! A. did two poses, one lying on my bed, and looked lovely. He was very tired and immediately fell asleep and snored! After that he had a thing for me to do for him and I was already when N. arrived. I had to slip on my dress over my bare skin & go to the door because A. didn't want to go down. So then the two of them drew. They both did good drawings. Then B. posed again. So we had a good evening of it. Do wish you could have been here.

Eleanor and Ruth moved to digs in Upper Mall which was close to Lyngard House, Austin's house on Chiswick Mall on the bank of the Thames. Lyngard House dated from the time of Queen Anne; it was very clean and in perfect taste, although Spartan, and painted throughout in broken white, Austin's favourite colour. He kept his own pictures modestly behind the sofa, turned to the wall. Austin hated pomposity – even his College nameplate with the title 'Professor' was hung on the lavatory door. He was a tall, good-looking and muscular man whose hair rose up strongly from his forehead; when Eleanor drew him, the hair on his head looked as if it were in flames. At the College he dressed immaculately in a well-cut suit, a white shirt with a stiff detached collar and an Italian silk tie. To those he liked he was pleasant, helpful, and immensely knowledgeable about his craft, but unassuming. To those he did not like he was cutting and he could also be silent or monosyllabic. At the same time 'Bob' Austin was also a 'ladies' man'. Women liked him. He could make himself agreeable and he enjoyed their admiration. Although twenty years his senior, Molly Bernhard-Smith from the XXI Gallery had been his lover and they continued to have an intimate relationship. He wrote to her: 'I do remember you getting a bit apprehensive about the old man [in the house next door] seeing you involved with a young man and without a stitch on him... There is no doubt, I may as well tell you, that I could do with a few nights in bed with you. Your fingers were the most delicate ever and too thrilling. When shall I ever feel them again?'[4]

Austin was seventeen years older than Eleanor. Having grown up for much of her life without a father of her own, she probably found in him a father figure. Charismatic and compelling, he overwhelmed Eleanor and she hero-worshipped him, but, more than that, like many girls before her she fell in love with her teacher. Since they lived so close, Ruth and she became part of the Austin household, and became friends not only with Robert Austin their teacher but also with his wife Ada and their children. As he was a very good and conscientious teacher who was always willing to help his female students, Ada was doubtless used to adoring young women and accepted this state of affairs: it was not a matter which they discussed in front of the family. She knew that had a girl ever caused any serious trouble she could have the girl dismissed from the College immediately. Ada led her own life. She was a classical scholar who had studied at Girton College, Cambridge, and wrote academic papers. Austin and she met in Rome when he had won a scholarship to the British School in Rome and they married in 1924. She also wrote books for little children which her husband illustrated. Within the household Eleanor, who was generous with her time, made evening dresses for Clare, the elder daughter, when she had not the money to buy expensive clothes. Rachel, her sister, was invited down to stay at Weston. Certainly Austin thought highly of Eleanor. For Christmas 1936 he gave her his engraving, 'Women Praying' inscribing it: 'To Eleanor Hudson with great admiration'. When he drew Eleanor she looks friendly, even coquettish, but it was not the drawing of a man in love.

The Austins had recently found and renovated a derelict chapel on the north Norfolk coast and turned what had been little more than four brick walls into a small house for holidays with a studio for painting. Burnham Overy Staithe was a little port. Horatio Nelson, who was born locally, had learned to row and sail at Staithe, and until the end of the First World War cargo had been shipped out from its tiny harbour which was barely more than a gap in the dunes but now Staithe was very quiet and very remote. The Old Chapel stood close to the water's edge. Beyond it there was nothing more than a deep ditch, an embankment and then marsh and tidal creeks and beach down to the sea, and above were endless skies and the sea-birds which Austin watched for hours. Staithe was where he painted his watercolours, rising very early in the morning and going out on his bike to sketch the landscape with just a flowerpot full of water dangling from the handlebars. In contrast to the painstaking meticulousness of his etching these Norfolk pictures were done quickly. They were very spare – often scarcely more than a few dashes of colour. He also did flower studies. Austin called these pictures his 'pot-boilers' because they were popular and always sold well but he was a perfectionist and he destroyed much of the work.

Students were invited up to Norfolk for sketching parties. Trains departed from Liverpool Street to Norwich, and at Norwich there was a connection to a branch line which wound its way around the Norfolk coast and included a stop at Burnham Market station, a couple of miles from Burnham Overy Staithe. Eleanor loved Overy Staithe and it made a deep impression on her. Some of her own rare landscapes were done there and they show that she had as much a facility for these as she had for figure studies. In 2009, more than fifty years after her last visit, Eleanor expressed her feelings for the place in a letter. She had been moved to write after reading some lines from Edward Thomas's poem, 'Adlestrop' which had been written during the First World War. The poet's train had halted unexpectedly at Adlestrop station in Gloucestershire:

Winter, Norfolk
watercolour, wash on blue-grey paper

Yes. I remember Adlestrop –
The name, because one afternoon
of heat the express-train drew up there
Unwontedly. It was late June.

The steam hissed. Someone cleared his throat.
No one left and no one came
On the bare platform. What I saw
Was Adlestrop – only the name.

Eleanor wrote:

> As I glanced over the Saturday Essay in our abominable D. Mail, it was caught by this name, which recalled a dim memory from long ago when I loved a strange little poem in a mixed book, no longer to hand - so I read on, recalling more, as it quoted one or two lines - and then remembered how it touched me, even more in bringing back my own experience of a tiny country station and the great loss and sadness induced by that meddling Dr Beeching in the banishing of beloved wee country stations. It recalled my happiest young days when I would visit a loved man on the wild coast of Norfolk - miles of dykes and creeks and heather with sand dunes at the end, and a thousand of wild rare birds, the sound of curlews crying, & such air, scents & freedom of space - So I travelled before Dr Beeching's day to a tiny, tiny station in countryside, the guard stepping off his train to blow the whistle and wave the flag, along with me stepping off, alone perhaps, to be met by him on his bicycle, one handed, the other hand skilfully manoeuvring a spare bike - then off for miles to the destination in that Paradise - What an aching-yearning when all that lovely simplicity of connection intimately with real air freedom (and flora and fauna?) was so brutally destroyed for all poor country people - and Me![5]

These, she continued were 'Experiences never lost in memory, sadnesses for lost things, people, places'. They were also a reminder of *Brief Encounter*, a film about unrequited love and much loved by her.

In May 1936 Eleanor and Ruth together with Bodil, Susan and Laurence all went on holiday to Norway. In the evenings they sat together playing bridge and reading while Eleanor and Ruth, who stayed in Norway a week longer, also spent time drawing. The holiday ended badly. Eleanor fell and damaged her already weak back. 'You must have been terrifically energetic, we shall never be able to make sarcastic remarks about your laziness now!' a friend wrote.[6] The fall must also have affected her heart for on her return to London Eleanor went into hospi-

Railway Carriage
watercolour, graphite

tal where she was not allowed visitors. She had flu-like symptoms, feeling 'groggy' with a sore throat and a temperature and her eyes were weak. From hospital Eleanor went into a nursing home in Knaresborough Place in South Kensington, and afterwards she was sent home to St Marychurch so that her mother could look after her. Meanwhile at the Royal College the other students continued with their exams which Eleanor was unable to take. The subjects for the engraving students to choose that year were 'The Road Menders', 'Dawn', or 'The Lost Piece of Silver', and they were also tested in wood-engraving, aquatint and mezzotint[7]. In reply to the letters from her friends Eleanor wrote reams about her frustration at having to stay in bed and about the flowers, the spring blossom and the birds in the garden at Weston. While she was away she had a picture called 'The Ball Dress' hung in the Royal Academy Summer Show which received a mention as a 'successful composition in etching' in *The Observer*.

A year later she missed yet more College. Once again the problem was her heart. She was able to do some work at home and Austin suggested to her, via Ruth, that her bedclothes might make a very good subject for a dry-point even if she had no-one to model for her. Instead Eleanor did a rare self-portrait. In the picture she sits up in bed with her head resting against three pillows and her legs covered by sheets. Her gaze is watchful and weary. It is unlike many of Eleanor's etchings in which she depicts versions of her own life: a girl leans across a dressing-table and gazes out of a window wondering what her future will bring; young women in pretty frocks sit in armchairs or at the table reading or mending and close by there is a lamp, a vase of flowers. She also made an uncharacteristic and very strange engraving called 'The Convalescent'. It is a mirror image of her self-portrait captured as if she were seeing herself caught in a nightmare: a girl lies in bed, her hair strewn wildly across the pillows, her eyes blazing; within the

Self Portrait in bed
etching

edge of the picture is the frame of a looking glass which stands on a set of drawers or a dressing table; in front of the glass branches wave uncontrollably. Eleanor never made another picture like it but its imagery belongs more to the world of Charles Dickens's illustrator George Cruikshank. Eleanor always seemed very much in control of her emotions but in this picture she could not be less so. Neither the self-portrait nor 'The Convalescent' was ever exhibited. Eleanor's prints are very different from those of Robert Austin, both in their technique – they make much more of shading – and in their subject matter. An etching called 'Lamplight' depicting a man trying to pick up a prostitute by the river at Hammersmith she described as an exercise in 'social realism' but mostly her work reflects the feminine domestic realities of her own world or of those she later observed in Italy. As she recovered Eleanor received a letter from Athol Hay at the Royal College reassuring her that it would be possible either to sit the examination at a later date or even be excused from the examination altogether if she had a doctor's certificate but she managed to return to the College to sit the examinations and by the time she graduated at the end of the summer term in 1937 Eleanor could claim to be a successful artist.

The Convalescent ***etching***

But the year ended badly. Merivale's home at Hoveton St Peter was close to Norwich and about thirty miles south-east of Burnham Overy Staithe. The thousands of apple trees he planted on his farm had to be maintained for six years before they were mature enough to bear fruit and return a significant profit. In the meantime Merivale grew dahlias and tomatoes which he sold around local shops and pubs. According to his letter heading he was a member of the National Dahlia Society and a 'Specialist in Hardy Fruit Culture and Horticulture'. He had a nice house, a wife Joan who had a maid – Joan was never allowed to work herself – and a baby daughter called Virginia with her own white pram. Merivale saw himself as a knight in white shining armour who had rescued Joan and her family from their disasters – his mother-in-law said he was a saint – and it was a life he loved. However his family were less happy and his brothers began to feel uneasy as to whether Merivale was using his money wisely. They looked at his accounts and seeing so little return for several years of outgoings, demanded to know whether he needed to employ so many men and whether he should not cut back on his expenditure. Merivale no doubt felt once again that he, the youngest brother, was being compared poorly with his more capable older brothers. He was not strong and he struggled from overwork, and the stress and constant worry affected his health. In early December 1937 he went into Norwich on business but he blacked out on his way to the railway station. After an hour and a half he walked into the house of a friend and immediately had a heart attack. The doctors told him to give up work and go away for six months' rest in a sunny climate. 'Of course all this is out of the question,' Merivale wrote to his mother. 'From now till Christmas I shall be making Holly Wreaths as hard as I can do... From the beginning of January until May is my busy time for propagating thousands of Dahlias.' Helen answered telling him not to worry. 'The problem will be looked at from every side. I have written to Joan that it is really a good deal like the time Eleanor went through at Easter, and Dr. Catford was right and wise to say "carry on".' Two days after Christmas Helen came into Eleanor's bedroom at seven o'clock in the morning and she lay down on Eleanor's bed which was not something she ever did. Confused and distressed, she told Eleanor that she had received a phone call to tell her that Merivale was dead. He had gone to bed the previous night, fallen into a coma and died. Prolonged anxiety had brought on heart failure. Laurence travelled up to Norfolk. He told his mother that in death his brother looked 'beautiful and peaceful'. Paige took the funeral service and Laurence played the organ. A year into its first crop of apples the farm at Hoveton St Peter had to be sold. Wanting to take Merivale's family under her wing, Helen had Joan, her mother, her three brothers and her young daughter move to St Marychurch where they bought a house, while Edmund became Virginia's guardian and looked after the family finances. The three surviving Hudson brothers never got over the episode. They felt in some way that they had let Merivale down and been responsible for his death. The affair was never talked about again within the Hudson family and his daughter Virginia did not hear the story of her father's life, and the circumstances of his death, until she asked Eleanor nearly seventy years later. Merivale, that 'very endearing chap', had been Eleanor's childhood playmate, the brother to whom she felt closest. His heart troubles and the manner of his death must have preyed upon her mind over the years.

Eleanor first showed in the Royal Academy Summer Exhibition in 1935 where she had two works, 'Lamplight' and 'The Kitchen', and she exhibited each year at the RA until 1940. In 1938 Brighton Museum and Art Gallery purchased 'Attic Bedroom' from the RA show. It was her first sale to a major British collection. By the end of the decade she had also exhibited in London and the provinces as well as in Canada, the USA and Scandinavia. She was a member of the Society of Artist Printmakers and the National Gallery of Canada bought an etching when they held an exhibition in Toronto. She was also a member of the Chicago Society of Etchers

River Wall, Lamplight
etching

H/c printer's proof

which, despite its name, was an international society, and in England Eleanor found a base at the Cooling Gallery[8], a commercial gallery in the Strand. In 1938 both Ruth and she were elected as Associate Members of The Royal Society of Painter-Etchers and Engravers. Until her election to the Society, Eleanor's name had always appeared in catalogues as 'Miss Eleanor E. Hudson'. Austin advised her that since there was still prejudice against women artists she should stand as 'Erlund' Hudson (Ruth stood as 'R. Aspden'). For most women who studied art there were only three choices: they married, they taught, or they worked as illustrators. It was still difficult for women artists not only to break through a masculine culture but also to have self-confidence when there were fewer opportunities for contacts and less chance to use presses and other necessary equipment. There was great surprise in the room when her name was called out in front of the Society as 'Mr Erlund Hudson' and the new Associate stood up and was revealed not to be a man at all. Her new name was a further sign of her growing independence and the identity she was creating for herself. From now on she remained Eleanor to those she knew personally but professionally she was always Miss Erlund Hudson.

The Royal Society of Painter Etchers and Engravers (the RE) exhibited with the Royal Watercolour Society (the RWS) which had its own galleries in Conduit Street in the West End. The galleries were situated in a former night club with one gallery downstairs and another above which had a metal balustrade around it. The red and white pillars, likened by someone to the colour of corned beef, divided the spaces between the columns into smaller areas. In 1939 Eleanor stood for election as an Associate of the Royal Watercolour Society, the second oldest artistic society in Great Britain after the Royal Academy. There were sixty-two candidates that year and Eleanor was nominated by Robert Austin and by Percy Jowett, another member of the College staff. She was – perhaps unexpectedly – elected while among the defeated candidates there were many far older and much more eminent artists than herself including members of other artistic societies. At 26 Eleanor became the youngest member of the RWS. There were only three full women Members: Dame Laura Knight, Eleanor Fortescue-Brickdale and Minnie Smythe, and three women Associates. All of the women in the Society were many years older than her and some were no longer exhibiting. Averil Burleigh, who was one of seven artists elected at the same time as Eleanor, first exhibited in 1912, the year Eleanor was born, and already had pictures in the collections of several provincial galleries. At her first show Eleanor exhibited three pictures – 'Woman Dressing', 'Restaurant' and 'Artist' – but unfortunately they were all hung upstairs in the less-favoured balcony gallery and they failed to sell.

Eleanor described her years at the Royal College as a period 'of joy and success'. After she received her diploma she was rewarded with a continuation scholarship for another year's study. Subsequently Helen discouraged her from applying to the College for the Rome Scholarship on the grounds that other students had greater financial needs and instead she applied for and received a travelling scholarship. The Board of Education in Whitehall sent her a form to fill in with information about her financial position. Eleanor wrote back to the Secretary setting out her position:

Dear Sir,

I apologize for not having replied to your letter with regard to the award of a R.C.A. Trav: Schol: which I am very happy to accept. I [am] uncertain how to fill up the enclosed form (GIOT.) with the necessary particulars of my financial circumstances. The form is apparently to be filled in by parents or guardian, but this presumably does not apply to me as I am independent of my parents, renting my own flat in London, & living on an independent (unearned) income. This income averages annually about £500. If a more detailed statement is necessary I will endeavour to look up the necessary papers, but I trust that the above information is sufficient for your purposes.

Yours faithfully,
E.E.H.[9]

The obvious country for travel was Italy. Eleanor had little interest in politics although her time at the Royal College coincided with the war in Spain about which she heard students arguing. Friends of Austin rescued Goya's etching plates from the Prado and arranged an exhibition of his engravings at the Victoria and Albert Museum. They only cost a few guineas and Eleanor later regretted missing the opportunity to buy one. She knew nothing about the situation in Italy however. Helen wanted Ruth to accompany Eleanor to Italy but Blackburn Education Authority, which had financed Ruth's studies at the RCA, wanted their loan to be repaid, circumstances which required her to start working as soon as possible. Eleanor's doctors also encouraged her to travel for the Italian climate could only be good for health. However there would be the inevitable hazards. A College friend warned her in advance:

The men here I divide into the following categories:
Pests - semi-pests & super-pests;
Loons - semi-loons & red-hot maniacs.
Stiffs - big stiffs & little stiffs +
Toughs & other oddments.
By now I am able - at a distance of approx. 30 Feet to place any approaching menace into his right category.

The children are divided up as follows:
The ear-drum piercers (who suddenly bellow when standing as close as possible to my ears)
The Torso-in-the-way placers.
The jog-elbowers (no apology)
The foreign-body carriers
The all-day leeches, etc., etc.,
I nearly forgot the dribblers and the no handkerchief brigade.[10]

For several months Eleanor travelled by bus or on foot around Rome, Lucca, Siena, and the northern cities. She must have lingered in Verona for several of her pictures have 'Verona' in their titles. She sketched the wine shops where she found digs, as well as the bars, the cafes, the flower-sellers, and the wash houses or *lavandarias*, all the places where men and, more especially, women gather together, drink and talk. There were very few foreigners to be seen but she enjoyed herself so much that she felt little need to care about the world beyond. Susan wrote to her mother-in-law, Helen, 'We are simply longing for news of Eleanor. We have no idea of her whereabouts, or when she is likely to be home. Do give us news of her.'[11] Eleanor was being elusive and when her mother urged her to come home because of the likelihood of war in Europe, Eleanor ignored Helen's increasingly anxious letters. In August 1939 however she stayed in a tiny hotel in the Dolomites. There were only three other guests, one of whom was a recuperating Italian naval officer. One morning in the dining room he lowered his newspaper, turned to her and ordered her fiercely, 'Signorina, go home!' She missed the outbreak of war by a couple of weeks.

1 EEH to Hugh Hudson, September 2001

2 A burin consists of a triangular or diamond-shaped steel rod 5 – 10 cm in length with a sharp tip. Fixed in a wooden handle it is pushed with the palm and guided with fingers to cut grooves in the copper plate.

3 The printer also controls the biting of the acid. A 15 minute bite resulting in fine lines would then be protected with varnish to prevent further biting before the plate is immersed in the acid for deeper bites. This process can be repeated for a couple of hours.

4 Robert Austin to Mollie Bernhard Smith, undated

5 EEH to Sarah Seymour, 28 February 2009

6 Joyce [?] to EEH, 14 May 1937

7 18th century techniques which Austin himself did not use.

8 J. Johnson and A. Greutzner, *The Dictionary of British Artists 1880 - 1940*

9 Copy in EEH's own archive

10 Denise Brown RE (1911 – 1998) to EEH and Ruth Aspden, undated

11 Susan Hudson to Helen Hudson, undated

Old Women (Italy)
graphite, pen and ink

Chapter Three – War Years

War had already been declared by the time the Royal Water Colour Society's Autumn Exhibition opened in October 1939. The Society hoped that visitors might be reassured about visiting the gallery by the fact that there was an official Air Raid Patrol shelter big enough for 150 people in its basement. Russell Flint, the President of the RWS, wrote to *The Times* regretting that since many galleries would have to close at dusk foggy days might present problems. On the other hand, he suggested, the fact that they were open at all during daylight hours could have a 'normalising' effect on the art-loving public.[1] However the public had other things on its mind than buying pictures and the exhibition had little success. After a month Eleanor's three watercolours – 'Girl Sewing', 'Under the Awnings' and 'Channel Crossing' – were once again unsold.

Matters were worse for the Royal Society of Painter-Etchers. For the whole course of the war the necessary tools and chemicals for print-making were in very short supply. Such was the Society's financial embarrassment that they agreed to include preliminary sketches in their exhibitions for the first time, and these were shown separately on the upper gallery. Eleanor produced four etchings and two studies for the show which opened early in 1940. Three of the etchings had 'Verona' in the title and she sold one of them at the exhibition but from now on her sketches and watercolours were always more successful. Two of her three works in the Royal Academy that summer – 'Interior, Verona' and 'Wineshop, Verona' – were apparently the same as those she had already shown earlier at the RE. Attendances slumped at the Academy too and Eleanor did not show again at the RA

Italian Flower Seller
etching

Wineshop, Verona
etching

until 1946. The RWS Galleries in Conduit Street suffered slight bomb damage so the Society's Autumn Exhibition was cancelled.

By early 1940 the unemployment rate for artists was recorded at 73 per cent.[2] Flint wrote again to the newspapers on the subject of finding work for artists. His suggestions included making more attractive black-out material: 'Why not design brown paper and black curtains with a cheerful pattern on the reverse or inner side?' A project called Recording Britain, financed by the Pilgrim Trust, was set up to record the nation's heritage. In the words of the art critic Herbert Read, the aim of the project was to show 'exactly what we are fighting for'[3], should there be losses either to German bombs or to post-war developers. However since

Eleanor and Robert Austin

Eleanor was not a topographical artist this was unsuitable work for her. Her weak back kept her out of any active war service so instead she was ordered to take part in suitable activities such as packing parcels for prisoners-of-war or serving in British War Canteens. This still gave her time for her art and financially she remained very much better off than many.

While Clare and Rachel Austin stayed on in Norfolk to attend the local school, their mother returned to live in London. In 1940 the Royal College of Art was evacuated to the safety of Ambleside in the Lake District where the students – who seemed startlingly bohemian to the locals – occupied the empty hotels. As well as being a teacher Robert Austin was an Official War Artist and he worked on a number of commissions between 1940 and 1944, beginning with a series of drawings of Coastal Command stations. He made a speciality of women's work: the Women's Royal Naval Service, Queen Alexandra's Military Nursing Service, and the Balloon Operators of the Women's Auxiliary Air Force. He also designed a series of London Transport posters for the Ministry of Information featuring portraits of British heroes such as Sir Francis Drake, Horatio Nelson, William Pitt and Winston Churchill.

No doubt Eleanor still saw Austin as often as she could. In Ruth's absence there was more chance for them to be alone together whenever he was in London, and somehow she came to believe – or she persuaded herself to believe – that her feelings for Bob, as she now called him, were returned in full. Among Eleanor's papers were found a number of photographs of Robert Austin both in his soccer kit and in the uniform of the Royal Garrison Artillery from his First World War service which she must have hoarded over the years. Yet whatever her feelings for him she did her best to keep them close to herself. In letters to Eleanor from friends he is scarcely mentioned, it is as if he were of no particular consequence in her life. Ruth, who would have known most, mentioned him only in passing, and even then he was always just 'Austin' never 'Bob'. Ruth was now working in a camouflage unit in Leamington Spa. She wrote to Eleanor about a recently married couple, Brian Reade, from St Marychurch, and his new wife Virginia Ware:

> I think you'd like them. She's rather sophisticated but not in a horrid way so don't be put off by that. She's only about 23 I think, rather tall and plump, does her hair up at the back and curls in front, very nice. I have not met him but Virginia says Brian would like to meet me as he has seen me about in London and St Marychurch for so long and the same with you. By the way she says Brian is not at all shy. Cherub, please burn or hide this from sight. Apparently they've lived together lots.[4]

She would have assumed that Eleanor had similar attitudes but if Eleanor was unable to share her feelings about Austin with Ruth then her burden must have been even heavier.

Coastal areas were officially forbidden to non-residents. Nevertheless Eleanor went to stay with the Austin family in Norfolk and was apprehended by a policeman who ordered her to appear in the local magistrates' court at Walsingham. The policeman told the court that Eleanor's defence was that a doctor had recommended the bracing air of the Norfolk coast whereas her home was already a seaside resort –Torquay. In the large empty court room Eleanor's own voice could scarcely be heard. However the bespectacled old magistrate told the policeman scathingly, 'Young man! Educated people know the difference between the enervating soft breezes of Devon and the real *bracing* air and restoring powers of Norfolk.' He fined Eleanor £1 and told her 'not to do it again'.[5] Her family was not greatly amused by this story. Laurence wrote from Cranbrook to his mother about Eleanor's evasiveness:

> It was absolutely grand to have visits from Edmund and Eleanor this term... Edmund was not questioned by coming into the area but even so would have been all right. I am terribly sorry Eleanor has to answer for going in the closed area in Norfolk. I gather she has not been home since leaving for Norfolk sometime ago. You must have found things very lonely without her for so long. I do hope you had a proper birthday celebration last Sunday.[6]

And then a few months later he wrote once more to Helen:

> Has Eleanor gone away again? I find it hard to keep track of her movements.[7]

In 1941 Eleanor did not exhibit with any Society. The whole of England seemed to be on the move. In his neat little handwriting Harry Philp, the Secretary to both the RWS and the RE, crossed out and rewrote the addresses of the artists and glued strips of paper into the back of an old catalogue as war uprooted many of the members from their homes. In London the owners of their digs in Upper Mall told Ruth and Eleanor that they wanted to empty their house for the duration of the war and take their children away for safety. In 1941 they both gave Lyngard House, the Austin's house, as a London address. Then for a short time they shared a tiny flat which Austin offered Eleanor in another house he owned in Weltje Road which was nearby and also ran down to the Thames. However after only a short time the Council requisitioned the property for locals who had lost houses in the bombing.

Meanwhile Edmund was fully occupied manufacturing essential supplies. He spent so much time travelling to London on ministry business that his mother referred to him as 'the

Women Making Bandages
watercolour, graphite

bachelor'. His home in Edinburgh became a haven for Norwegian relatives fleeing German occupation or on leave during active service. Laurence, who was the Director of Music at Cranbrook School in Kent, served in the Home Guard. On Sunday mornings he played at the local parish church St Dunstan's in his hobnailed boots, ready to go out on parade immediately afterwards. From 1 November 1941 onwards, Philp recorded that Eleanor's address was now Ashby Magna Vicarage in Leicestershire, a rural parish between Leicester and Rugby, where Paige was now the vicar.

Paige was seven years older than his sister. Following disagreement with the headmaster of Milner Court School he had left the school. Needing a new job Paige went to a theological college and retrained for the Anglican priesthood; after curacies in London and Birmingham he was given the Leicestershire living. His parishioners saw in their new vicar a fit young man who was available for heavy jobs; as well as having to tend to parish affairs, local schools and the religious needs of his parishioners he was expected to mend roofs and heave coals. With two small children of their own Paige and his wife Susan were also looking after evacuees in their large, rambling vicarage. Susan was now pregnant again so, needing all the help they could get, Eleanor was called on to stay with them. In September 1942 she was present at the birth of Susan's daughter who was christened Helen Myrth Bergitta.

As well as working in the vicarage, pumping water, and looking after the hens which always seemed to lay their eggs in the midst of great holly bushes, Eleanor travelled into Leicester for her war work. But in every spare hour there were subjects to be painted: 'Always for me it involved human activities – here were for me such interesting events which later became a series of my watercolours of "women doing voluntary war work". It was a kind of war work but it was mainly for my own pleasure.'[8] These activities provided ideas and themes for pictures: forces canteens where women worked in the kitchen amidst many-coloured arrangements of sinks, towels and mixing-bowls, and airmen in greatcoats sitting in the canteen. Eleanor's great love of materials and of the shapes they formed now found another role. She made many studies of members of the Women's Voluntary Service (the WVS) as they spread sheets of cloth such as sheets given for war supplies and then cutting them up for bandages or pyjamas. Ashby Magna itself was a source for another series of drawings. The vicarage had large outlying barns where the country women dried festoons of wild flowers and herbs which they hung from the beams like decorations, and then prepared them on trestle tables for the local hospitals. Eleanor loved the way in which light reflected upwards through its low windows into the wooden rafters. These were some of her favourite pictures. 'I think that artists can see in all kinds of circumstances and conditions, design and beautiful compositions whatever the subject,'[9] she said. They were to be both the first watercolours which sold and ultimately the pictures which she regarded as of most lasting significance.

In the middle of January 1943 Eleanor went down to London for the Royal Society of Painter-Etchers exhibition after which she spent six weeks at home in Torquay. The time gave her an opportunity to prepare works for forthcoming exhibitions. In her pocket diary, among birthdays and the concert performances she listened to on the radio, she recorded her intense

Peeling Potatoes, WVS Canteen
graphite

Peeling potatoes
Canteen

delight in the natural world and the coming of spring:

11 February

> Saw 5 bullfinches (male) in one small almond tree blossoms just opening.

12 February

> First daffodils at Weston

16 February

> Pair of rooks flying to elms with twigs.

17 February

> Blackbirds singing well - male and female, bullfinch pair feeding together in bushes outside bedroom window.[10]

But for her birthday on February 18th she recorded just one word: 'dentist'. By early March Eleanor was back in Leicestershire where the flowers were not as advanced as those in Torquay – 'Ashby Magna – crocuses & snowdrops, daffs in bud only. Primroses violet buds'. Despite her deep love of flowers, they appear as incidental features in Eleanor's pictures, in a vase in a composition or as a part of a rare still life. It was only near the end of her life that she made them the main subject of the work.

For the duration of the war the National Gallery took down its paintings and sent them for safe storage to the Manod slate quarry near Blaenau Ffestiniog in Wales. In order to fill the empty galleries the pianist Myra Hess began lunchtime concerts which the public could attend for a shilling. They were immensely successful and sometimes drew an audience of over a thousand people. A group of ladies volunteered to do the catering and their sandwiches came to be known as the best in London. Seeing the success of the concerts Kenneth Clark, the Director of the National Gallery, suggested to the Ministry of Information that they set up a War Artists Advisory Committee. The official intention of the Committee was propaganda, organising exhibitions to promote Britain's image at home and abroad. In reality, Clark said later, 'my aim, which of course I did not disclose, was simply to keep artists at work on any pretext, and, as far as possible, to prevent them from being killed.'[11]

The Gallery organised a wide range of exhibitions and they proved popular with the public who came in large numbers to see them. Those for 1943 included 'Ballet Design' and 'Greater London: Towards a Master Plan'. 'War Pictures by British Artists' exhibitions had been held there each year of the war from 1940 onwards, and Robert Austin suggested to Eleanor that

Drying Herbs
graphite, pen and ink, watercolour

she send some of her drawings to the Ministry of Information for their consideration. A week later at the beginning of May she heard to her surprise that they had agreed to buy six pictures for twenty-five guineas and hang them as part of that year's show. Four of the drawings were on similar themes: 'WVS Cutting-Out Pyjamas for WAAF', 'WVS Cutting Calico for Emergency Cots' and two versions of 'WVS Bandage-Making'. They are all confident and ambitious white-on-white compositions, full of different shapes and rhythms, in which the WVS women – in their white uniform looking like nurses or nuns – hold out stretches of white fabric ready for cutting. The Ministry also purchased one of her Ashby Magna watercolours, 'Country-women Drying Herbs', and 'Forces Canteen Kitchen'. In the latter there are six women at work in a narrow kitchen; one is filling a water jug from an urn while the others are busy with mixing bowls. The ladies who were doing the catering at the National Gallery must have been part of a similar scene.

At the end of May 1943, Paige and Susan went to St Marychurch for a weekend away from the parish while Ruth came to stay with Eleanor at Ashby Magna. Already the previous week there had been Luftwaffe attacks on Bournemouth and Brighton. Torquay was to be their third target. The pilots were told to aim for gas works, railways and factories which included an Aircraft Works in St Marychurch, and the large hotels many of which had been requisitioned by the RAF. However such was the intensity of the anti-aircraft fire and the concentration of the hills around Torquay that the young German pilots dropped their bombs as soon as they could. They were just concerned with staying alive and getting home as safely as they could. In consequence St Mary's, the parish church, received a direct hit killing twenty-one Sunday School children and three teachers. Only the church tower was left standing with its clock standing at twenty minutes to three while the rest of the church was razed. An aircraft struck off the nearby spire of the Catholic Church of Our Lady Help of Christians and the pilot crashed into the Teignmouth Road where he was killed, along with many others that afternoon. People came out of their houses to help bringing bath tubs, clothes baskets, anything to carry away the rubble. A chain of helpers, many of them young RAF men in shorts and singlets, passed the loads of debris back. Great lumps of masonry were pulled down with ropes in order to clear paths out of the ruins and through the window and door spaces. It was estimated that some five hundred tons of rubble were shifted during the afternoon and evening. The nuns from the local convent brought out urns of tea for the workers.

The Torquay Times likened the Rogation Sunday attack to the bombing of Guernica and Abyssinia:

> From such men, in the hour of their frustration, we can only expect every bestial deed and vengeful method of attack. Their cold inhumanity was, and is, the most terrible indictment of their system.

The Herald Express recorded how one of the workers marvelled as the surviving children were brought out alive they did not cry. 'They behaved like English children,' he said. The news was also broadcast overseas by the BBC.[12]

Weston, less than fifty yards away from the church, was very badly damaged and all the windows in the house and the conservatory were smashed. Paige and Susan were in bed resting after lunch. It was a small compensation but to his relief Paige's glasses – without which he could scarcely see – were found unharmed among the sheets. Eleanor's response to the horrors of war was that she could not bring herself to paint any of it. She insisted that art was for life not death. She remarked once that it was difficult to define ugliness; but it was surely here.

Over the next weeks at Ashby Magna Eleanor continued to record the activities of the hens and their eggs and the comings and goings of the birds in the garden. In her diary she makes no mention of the strains within the house yet they were increasing, somehow they were even in the garden:

10 June

3 eggs

Greenfinch young robbed by rook (in holly)

11 June

3 eggs

Flycatchers hatch (yew tree in churchyard)

15 June

Flycatcher's nest in thorn tree in the yard, young - saved blackbirds from cat, outside room

Blackbirds left nest outside room in evening

18 June

Blacky broody

2 eggs

Flycatchers in yew destroyed (cat?)[13]

On the 23rd of the month she recorded RSA [Robert Sargent Austin]'s birthday. At the end of the month Eleanor went away for a couple of days. On her return, her diary entry for Saturday July 3rd reads: 'Susan went to Warwick N[ursing] Home.' She had suffered a severe nervous breakdown.

Susan had many problems. She was stressed from overwork in her home and in her work. She had deprived herself of her rations in order to feed her growing family. The St Marychurch bombing can only have made matters worse. At a deeper level, Susan had a problem with Paige's family and felt shy with them. She never felt comfortable staying at Weston. Her mother was a milliner; her father had been a soldier in the Boer War who had taken to gambling and spent time in prison in Durban in South Africa; his wife left him and returned to England while he later went to Australia where he had made a bigamous second marriage. Susan spent seven months in the nursing home. During her time in Warwick she was kept sedated; whenever she woke up she was immediately put back to sleep again. This was thought the best cure. It was finally understood however that her main problem was that she could not cope with having Eleanor in her house. Eleanor and Paige were close and understood one another well. Paige always took Eleanor's side and she rather tactlessly took charge of Paige and the running of his home. Like her sister Elizabeth, Eleanor was bossy and Susan no longer felt in charge of her own home.

A psychotherapist interviewed Susan and he told Paige that she could return home only after Eleanor had left. In later years Eleanor and Susan became very fond of one another – they had many artistic interests in common – but Eleanor never completely forgave herself for the harm she had done.

In Susan's absence Eleanor had to give up her work in Leicester and she learnt to cook from the farmers' wives although she said that she was never much good at it. In July she went up to London again and at the National Gallery she heard a brilliant young Australian pianist called Noel Mewton-Wood play piano sonatas by Weber and Schubert. A couple of weeks later she went to Burnham Overy Staithe for three nights. It was her first visit for a couple of years. The short holiday must have been a pleasure and a relief although when she returned to Leicestershire she found that one of the chickens had been killed by a fox.

Fortunately the difficult situation came to a close. Laurence and his wife Linda were due to have their third child at the beginning of October. It was arranged that Eleanor should go down early and help with the birth regardless of the problems, not least of which was the fact that Cranbrook was in the path of the German flying bombs – 'doodle bugs' – on their way to London. She was also going to have to take with her Myrth, who was now nearly twelve months old and crawling. The journey was a nightmare as they travelled by the milk train in the early hours of the morning through blacked-out railway stations, from the Midlands down to London, then across London to take another train to Kent. When they reached Cherry Tree Cottage the house was already in darkness. The following night, when Eleanor was still exhausted from her journey, there was a terrible storm. Linda started to go into labour three weeks early and Laurence, in his dressing gown, went to rouse Eleanor from her bed. The doctor refused to come out because of the torrential rain, and so Eleanor, who had been present when Myrth was born and therefore had some idea what to do, delivered the baby herself. Meanwhile Laurence headed off his five-year old son Hugh who was woken by the thunder-

Railway Lines under Snow, Earls Court
oil on board

storm and marched out of his bedroom demanding to see his mother. He also heated up a huge kettle of water on a small methylated spirit stove although by the time the water boiled his new baby daughter had already been born. Eleanor always said that delivering her niece Sarah at midnight on September 13th was her finest achievement of the war.

She stayed on for a while longer and at the end of the month there was a small party to celebrate Myrth's first birthday. Eleanor wrote to 'Pasu' (as she called Paige and Susan), 'I suppose she didn't understood much about it, she did enjoy her parcels (esp: the wrapping paper!) and the candle on her cake.'[14] Myrth was returned to Ashby Magna where her brothers were being looked after by ladies in the village and Eleanor went back to London. From the middle of September onwards there are very few entries in her diary. In London there were neither hens, nor birds nor wild flowers and her life was soon fully occupied in other ways.

Eleanor moved into digs on the fourth floor of No. 6 Knaresborough Place. Cousin Violet lived at No. 2. She had married for the first time at the age of 61 but been widowed only three years later. Ruth, who was now married and called Ruth Rutter, was living in Hogarth Road nearby and Eleanor helped with her new baby daughter and found time to draw studies of the mother and child. The new flat was in a tall building off the Earls Court Road overlooking the lines of the District Railway as far as the South Kensington museums. The coming and going of the trains below made the flat very noisy but the air sirens were still heard above the roar. She could also sit up in bed where she could see the direction of the flying bombs as they approached from the south east. If they were coming towards her she had to run down a hundred stairs to the basement shelter. She painted the view from her window: a small oil painting from that time she described as a 'good study in straight lines'[15]. In the picture some of the tall buildings have been deliberately cut away to make room for the curves of the railways which are such a dominant feature of the landscape near the busy Earls Court junction. After the war the land was extensively developed and the railway lines coming out of Earls Court now run under tunnels. The image remains a rare topographical record.

As Eleanor could drive she was asked to help at an emergency centre at Notting Hill Gate. She was provided with an old converted laundry-van with a big horn which she drove around the local bombsites to wherever people were digging among the debris. As victims and rescuers struggled from under the ruined buildings and the fogs of plaster dust Eleanor handed out tea and sandwiches. Sometimes she was called on to do two shifts, one straight after the other, and had to continue working into the middle of the night. She saw the horrors of war: when the Troy Court flats were half destroyed by the bombing there were bodies and limbs strewn everywhere. A young American serviceman came up to her van and said to Eleanor, 'Oh ma'am, let me help dry cups.' He was white with shock from having carried out so many of the dead. The van reminded him of home and he spent the whole day with her. 'We all went about London and did everything one could in a most normal way,' Eleanor said. 'One was more alive because of the circumstances, more vital – even though outwardly calm, much of the time everyone was terrified of course.' All the same in London despite everything there

Ruth Rutter, mother and child
graphite

was no feeling of danger from people at large. The true danger came from machines.

In the air-raid shelter she used with Ruth and her baby she came to know a little family of refugees who had managed to escape from Czechoslovakia with what little they could in suitcases and bundles. The group consisted of two sisters who were barristers, their husbands, and their younger brother, Eugene, a medical student. The family became good friends but they were very bewildered by the way in which the British stayed calm as the fire bombs dropped around them while they tore to and fro trying to save their few precious belongings. Bella, one of the Czech women, became a favourite model for Eleanor and she posed for her wearing her national dress.

After such a long, dismal period the Royal Watercolour Society was thriving. The Spring Exhibition of 1943 had increased its sales by forty per cent but the following year the exhibition was even more successful. It was as if the public were exhausted by deprivation and anxiety and had decided to spend what spare money there was on its pleasures, and that included the arts. The RWS Spring Exhibition of 1944 was the most successful show for fifteen years. Eleanor exhibited three pictures, 'Girl Reading' and 'Girl in a Green Smock' and a war picture, 'Canteen Kitchen'. The exhibition toured to Sheffield where 'Girl in a Green Smock' was bought for twelve guineas by a local collector who bought five more pictures from the same show.

When she could Eleanor went down to St Marychurch where she rented a large spare room in a house on Torquay cliff tops as a studio. It had views across Torbay and sometimes she saw air combats. Weston remained very badly damaged, its windows broken and boarded up for the duration of the war. However Elsie the maid still polished the silver and Padden still tended the Weston garden. Eleanor drew her mother often. Indomitable but now silver-haired and rather frail, she spent a lot of time in her rocking-chair. She was very deaf and used a hearing-aid shaped like a trumpet. Helen also continued to type long letters and in May 1944 she wrote at length to tell Paige that she had sent him gooseberries from the garden and Edmund a box of lettuces. Churchill had allowed garden flowers to be sent by rail because he believed it was good for morale and she sent violets to Eleanor and to Violet who was staying with her:

> Today the consignment was sweet peas and as it was early closing they had to be posted by the noon post so I hope the longer time in the post office won't make too much difference in their freshness. They did look lovely when Padden brought them in this morning fresh picked, but then alas! I could not get them off by the first post as there was not a box in the house to take them! He had inquired on the way up at two shops for possible booty in the way of boxes but no go. Later smiling Mrs. Avery saw the difficulty and marched out to Fore Street and returned triumphant with a pile of 3 or 4 of various sizes got from Miss Dagworthy, one of which you had though it was too late for the morning-post. Elsie was convulsed at the vision of Mrs. A hidden behind her assortment as she came along, and in view of her short stature I imagine it was

Bella
graphite

> rather comical... If you want to telephone any evening I am of course usually in, but if no answer comes it may be I have trotted over to the post so try again later. There is a perfectly lovely thing on tonight being beautifully played by the Gersham Parkington Quintette.[16] It penetrates my type-clicking (Massenet), and just now I have been listening to "Ralph"[17] I suppose in a delightful concert. Unfortunately I can't stop to listen to these things except through my jobs. However I did stop for the Raymond Swing broadcast from U.S.A. as he is always worth listening to and was very interesting tonight about the set-to at the Racketeers in New York clearing up crime. He says the extraordinary crime wave is on the wane.[18]

In London the bombing continued into the final year of the war, and yet, oddly, there were good things too. In September 1944 when the trees in Earls Court were so shaken in a bombing raid that every leaf seemed to be blown off, a layer of dust settled. Then the leaves came back again so it was as if there were another spring in the late summer. 'It gave one hope,' Eleanor said. As the raids grew fewer, as 1945 arrived Eleanor was increasingly free from her commitments. She moved into Lovell House, one of her mother's properties, and divided her time between St Marychurch, Torquay and Knaresborough Place in London. In her diary she mentions going to see *St Joan* in Hammersmith with Ruth, a performance of Czech dance a few days later, and then on March 10th Myrna Loy and William Powell in *The Thin Man*. The first blackbird of the year had started singing in Knaresborough Place and the pigeons were building their nests. In April she took the train to Burnham Market to stay with 'my dear friends on the coast of Norfolk. Robert "Si" Austin, he my former teacher (wonderful)... in their creek-side cottage at B-o-S. It had become for me in its then wild state the most wonderfully beautiful (yet stark!) place in England.'

Eleanor drew Bella frequently in the last weeks of the war. Bella left for Prague on the last day of May 1945, very shortly after the end of the war in Europe full of hope for the future and the incoming government. Within a couple of years however the Communists had completely taken over and she openly expressed her disillusion and unhappiness. They shot her. Eleanor later made a note in her diary: 'Was it true she died in Prague – very young – 2-3 years later.' When Micu her husband saw the drawings Eleanor had made he was overcome. He covered them with kisses, crying, 'It's her, it's her.'

1 Simon Fenwick, *The Enchanted River*, 2002

2 David Mellor, Gill Saunders and Patrick Wright, *Recording Britain A Pictorial Domesday of Pre-War Britain*, 1991

3 ibid

4 Ruth Aspden to EEH, 24 April 1941

5 EEH memoir

6 Laurence Hudson to Helen Hudson, July 1941

7 Laurence Hudson to Helen Hudson, November 1941

8 IWM interview recording, 1983

9 IWM ibid

10 EEH, pocket diary 1943

11 Suzanne Bosman, *The National Gallery in Wartime*, 2008

12 Iris Origo, *War in the Val d'Orcia*, 1947

13 EEH, pocket diary 1943

14 EEH to Paige and Susan Hudson, October 1943

15 IWM ibid

16 The Gersham Parkington Quintette, a household name, played light music on the radio.

17 Possibly a reference to Ralph Nicholson, a musician friend and contemporary of Laurence Hudson

18 Helen Hudson to Paige Hudson, May 1944

Chapter Four – London 1945–1954

As life returned to some sort of normality Eleanor left her mother Helen with others looking after her and she went back to London where she enthusiastically re-entered its thriving art scene. Elizabeth and her family returned to England for the first time in seven years and bought a house in St Marychurch called The Hermitage. Helen's two sisters had both died many years beforehand and she had not been back to New England since the christening of the four elder children in 1907. She yearned to see her family and the sites of her youth but in 1948 she sent Eleanor in her place. Eleanor called the trip an 'Après-Guerre Holiday'. She had to sign pledges that Elizabeth would support her entirely since travel restrictions meant that she could only take £5 out of the country for her return taxi-travel expenses in England. For three months she travelled around Boston and Ogunquit on the Atlantic Coast of Maine staying with her sister's family and her innumerable young cousins. She also took some of her prints in her suitcase for sale in order to help pay for the visit and the Museum of Fine Arts in Boston bought four etchings for its collection.

In October, not long after Eleanor's return to England, her mother died from a stroke. She was seventy-six. As the church was still in ruins – it was not rebuilt for several years – the funeral took place in the parish hall which was known as 'Little St Mary's'. *The Torquay Times* published a long obituary and report of the funeral under the heading 'Playing Fields Advocate'. Weston was put up for sale with its shattered windows still boarded up. Eleanor said it was like a slum inside and complained that she had been left to clear its contents. The house was bought by a builder and divided into two. A wall was built down the middle of the big lawn where the Hudson children had played tennis and croquet, the conservatory was dismantled, and over the course of time bungalows took over the vegetable garden. Eleanor continued to go back to Torquay for a few years longer but then she sold Lovell House and Torquay ceased to be part of her life.

The trust which Helen's father Peder Olsen set up for his three daughters forty years earlier was now dissolved. It had successfully weathered the upheavals of the stock market over the decades and this long period of investment meant that Eleanor now inherited significant private means. Wisely re-invested, these would provide funds for the next sixty years of her life. But first of all she wanted to find a house of her own in London. She said that her short experience of living in Weltje Road made her long to live beside the river; now at last she had the means to buy a house of her own. Over dinner one night Robert Austin heard that No. 6 Hammersmith

Terrace was for sale by its owners, Eliot Hodgkin, a manager for Imperial Chemical Industries, and his wife, Katherine. The Hodgkins were not particularly artistic but a picture hanging over a mantelpiece in the house, 'a doubtful watercolour by David Cox' given to them as a wedding present, made their young son Howard decide when he was only five that he wanted to become an artist:

> I became aware... of pictures as things like tables, chairs, cups and saucers and so on. That conviction about the nature of pictures has perhaps saved me, helped me and protected me ever since.[1]

Mrs Hodgkin had taken her children to the United States during the war and the house was now shabby and neglected. Inside its walls were a strange yellowish colour and the doors had been painted in all sorts of different colours by the young Howard Hodgkin. Nevertheless Hammersmith Terrace was precisely what Eleanor was looking for and she used the £9000 she received as her portion of the sale of Weston to acquire the house. Then she bought lots of pots of white emulsion and painted it throughout. (Although she used to make a joke that had she known how valuable Hodgkin's paintings were to become she would have left the doors as they were and sold them off separately.) From the outside the row of narrow, many-storied houses was rather plain and austere. Originally the fronts of the houses had been the backs for Hammersmith Terrace had faced onto the river. When the Terrace was built in the 1760s the Thames was low enough for a horse and carriage to pass between the house and the river; then over the years as the tides increased the houses were remodelled and turned to face the road. At No. 6, which had four-storeys and a basement, a Victorian porch with narrow Gothic columns was added. Many artists and writers had lived along this short reach of the Thames. Edward Johnston, the father of modern British calligraphy, lived at No. 3. No. 7 had been the home of William Morris's friend the typographer and antiquary Emery Walker and the house remained fully furnished in Morris's Arts and Crafts style. Sir Alan Herbert, or A.P. Herbert as he was known, the author, humorist and MP, was still living at No. 12. Each of these men was eventually commemorated under the London Blue Plaque scheme.

No. 6 Hammersmith Terrace was Eleanor's home for more than fifty years and she loved it all. She took great pleasure filling it with Staffordshire china, Siamese cats, pictures and all manner of objects – most of which, for Eleanor, would have their own stories. On the ground floor there was a large sitting room with her baby grand piano and books and photographs. The room faced south down the garden and across the Thames. Its walls were painted a pale green so that the garden might seem to enter inside the house and at night the ripples from the Thames were reflected in the milk white ceiling. Eleanor's studio was on the first floor. Cupboards had been fitted along one wall and above them she hung a set of

Low Tide, Hammersmith Bridge
watercolour

Low Tide at Hammersmith Terrace

prints by Marc Chagall, an artist she loved. The bedrooms were decorated in light colours with delicately patterned material; the curtains were soft and pretty and floated against the open windows. There were Persian mats on the old floorboards and all the woodwork was painted white. Always there were pictures on the walls but singly and never crowded. From the top of the house the views were splendid with Hammersmith Bridge on the left and Chiswick Eyot to the right. The garden stretched below, at the end of which there was a wall. On the flood tide on the night of January 31st and the early hours of February 1st 1953 the River Thames rose so high that it almost breached the wall itself and at its full height at 4.00am it was only two inches from the top. Eleanor wrote in her diary that the moon was so full that it was not like night at all.

'Life with the arts!' Eleanor wrote, 'guests enjoying, art, music and literary neighbours.'[2] The house was ideal for parties. She enjoyed entertaining and her Oxford and Cambridge Boat Race parties were great affairs although, as with all her parties, guests were often invited spontaneously and at the last moment. One evening a well-known pianist arrived on her doorstep during a party. He was ushered in and sat down at the piano and began to play, joined by Eleanor who was a fine pianist herself. After an hour or more he asked where his hostess was. He had come to No. 6 by mistake, having actually been invited to another party a few doors away. This air of eccentricity was typical of the house. It was as if anything might happen.

Now that she had found a house Eleanor needed someone to look after it. She employed Mrs Laurie as a housekeeper, a large, kindly woman without much formal education who had spent her whole life in domestic service. The arrangement almost came to grief at the start. After a week she walked one day into the studio where a model was posing nude. Shocked, Mrs Laurie resigned immediately, telling Eleanor she had not realised that she had come to work in 'that sort of household'. Eleanor, which was very unusual for her, burst into tears and pleaded with her to stay for just one more week. One week turned into twenty-nine years and she stayed until she died, mothering Eleanor, always able to help, provide tea or a meal, wash up, or do some ironing. Eleanor in return helped pay to educate Mrs Laurie's daughter who subsequently married a wealthy businessman. As a result Mrs Laurie no longer needed to work but such was her devotion to Eleanor that even after visits to her daughter she would still return to Hammersmith Terrace driven by her son-in-law's chauffeur in his Rolls Royce. Eleanor always had the ability to find and adopt stray people because of their qualities and give them work within their capacities. Among her 'finds' was a tiny, timid lady called Miss Smith who often stayed in the house in order to do the household sewing. Another member of her household was Joan Skinner, a cockney who was brought up in an orphanage and had a very limited experience of life. Joan became one of her models and, like anyone who worked for Eleanor, was encouraged by her to appreciate the arts and music. Nevertheless Eleanor wrote to Paige:

> my own [house] is one that I barely keep chin above water in because I'm stubborn about not surrounding myself with the fleet of full-time cooks, maids, chauffeurs, secretaries that would make life so simple (& dull!).[3]

Eleanor enjoyed organising. With Hammersmith Terrace as her base she became a sort of universal aunt to many children as they passed through London, driving them around in her Rover saloon to take them to the station and put them on their trains. She took pride in knowing all the short cuts and always beating taxis at lights. As well as four of her nephews who were travelling to Marlborough, Eleanor also looked after a solemn little boy called Peter Cook on his way to Radley College. Cook, who was later to become famous as an actor and satirist, was the son of Madge Mayo, one of Eleanor's oldest friends. Madge and she had both attended St Winifred's School in Torquay forty years earlier. In 1953 at the Coronation Eleanor stayed at home and held a party for her friends in front of the television but sent off her three nephews Michael, Alan and John with a packed lunch prepared by Mrs Laurie to take their places in the crowds of the Coronation procession.

In her general business transactions Eleanor assumed – wrongly – that she lacked business acumen, and she was willing to trust the judgement of others. She believed that money should be used to good effect and to this end she was enormously generous. (Eventually even the various sums in her very inclusive will were allotted with regard to the

Mrs Laurie

Eleanor photographed by Lotte Meitner-Graf

amount of good they might do.) As her mother had done before her, Eleanor invested in property, and she began by buying the Hammersmith Terrace garages. Although an investment which brought a steady annual income, they also provided parking facilities for her neighbours and friends. The enterprise was dear to her heart and she was always ready to help the people who rented them. Her agents protectively drew up a licensing agreement which had to be signed every year. When one of her tenants asked whether, although it went against the wording of the agreement, he could keep a boat and household furniture and goods there instead of a car she readily agreed. Each year, with her explicit approval, he altered the wording by hand to this effect before signing it. Again like her mother Eleanor had an interest in architecture and house conversions. She revised the building plans for the Little Red House in Hasketon, a village outside Woodbridge in Suffolk, and in 1953 she went frequently to oversee building work at the house which belonged to a friend, an attorney called Helen Marriott.

Eleanor stayed at the Little Red House on New Year's Eve 1954. Although unwell she went down to the drawing room in her dressing gown at midnight to drink everyone's health for the coming year. On the same first page of her diary for the New Year she recorded her weight: on the seventh of September 1953 she weighed ten stone, two pounds; on the third of October she weighed ten stone, six pounds. Always very conscious of her appearance, Eleanor had a number of photographs taken by Lotte Meitner-Graf, a fashionable Austrian photographer who had a studio in Bond Street. She was pictured in a variety of poses and costumes: working on a copper plate or standing in a low-cut evening dress with jewels around her throat. She was disappointed by them however and made a note:

> Sorry, cannot bear them mostly - All too fancy and self conscious - My fault in allowing - Also some heads foreshortened - too big at top.[4]

Perhaps she thought they were not exactly 'her'. It was more typical of Eleanor that on one occasion after a few hours gardening – she was forever re-potting petunias – she should have absent-mindedly turned up for a performance at Covent Garden in an evening dress and jewellery but with a pair of gardening shoes on her feet. Among Eleanor's photographs there were

Seated Nude
conté crayon, graphite

a few nude and semi-nude negatives of her sitting by herself on a pebbly beach, and she also made a nude self-portrait in watercolour wash. Many years had passed since she told Sir William Rothenstein that she thought that the idea of a nude model was indecent.

In the post-war years Eleanor was busy working and exhibiting again. Between 1946 and 1953 Eleanor showed eleven etchings and ten drawings at the annual exhibitions of the Royal Society of Painter-Etchers and Engravers. Two of her drawings were bought, one for nine guineas, the other for eight guineas, but none of her etchings – which were much cheaper – sold. However as sales of prints began to pick up and the equipment needed for making them more available, such preparatory drawings were no longer allowed into the Society's shows. Eleanor's last engravings – 'Dancers' Dressing Room', 'Dancer and Rocking Chair', and 'Dancer and Dressers' – were exhibited in 1953 but these too were unsuccessful and from then on Eleanor effectively withdrew from the Society.

She was much more actively engaged with the Royal Watercolour Society, and from 1947 onwards she generally had at least three works in both the Spring and Autumn Exhibitions. Also in 1947 her work was chosen to participate in a British Council Travelling Exhibition. In 1951 and 1952 Eleanor was elected a member of the RWS Council although she said later that at the time she was still 'very naïve'. Sir William Russell Flint had been President of the Society since 1936 and he ran the Society together with Harry Philp, a rather uninspiring man with a perpetual 'dewdrop' at the end of his nose, who had been Secretary for nearly fifty years. (Eleanor was on the Council when the Society's wonderful watercolour drawing by John Sell Cotman was unfortunately, and unnecessarily, sold to the picture dealer Agnew's for £500 in order to redecorate the Gallery.) Matters did not improve in the administration of the RWS until Robert Austin became a very effective President of the Society in 1956 and cleared out much of the obstruction. His first action was to sack the hapless Philp.

Eleanor's work had developed through phases. The typical early Erlund Hudson picture was an interior scene of female life, the world she herself knew intimately. It had a title such as 'The Mirror', 'Fireside', 'Girl with a Book', or 'Woman Brushing Her Hair'. Later there came her Italian scenes, then her war pictures and subsequently the ballet work. While the similarities in their sketches are evident, Austin's influence only rarely extended to the composition of her pictures. In her etchings she never achieved his clarity and distinctiveness of line and her figures are never arranged, as his often are, in a frieze almost without depth. In her watercolour drawings her most significant influence were the Impressionists, particularly Degas, whose naturalistic, every-day subject matter was sympathetic to her and made for colourful pictures. Most of all, Eleanor was deeply interested in the narrative of life. Whatever she etched or sketched or painted in watercolours, her pictures were not just compositions but expressions of her curiosity about life, about story-telling, and overwhelmingly her fascination with people. In the rather decorous language of its time a critic for *Art News and Review* said of one of her pictures in the 1950 RWS Spring show:

Self-portrait, Nude
watercolour

> The charm of water colours is their eternal freshness. They have the dewy complexion of a summer's day that lingers in one's thoughts, and their speech is graceful rather than emphatic; their tone pure and unhampered by secrets... But a delightful literary painting by Miss Erlund Hudson called ***The Letter*** keeps one guessing as to its contents, and they cannot be ignored since the design is woven around that slight piece of paper. A girl kneels on the floor reading her letter. She has hurriedly flung her frothy ballet dress and white bouquet upon the old iron bedstead; a vertical plane running behind her pyramid pose. The colour of subtle limpid greens, greys and blues, with a dot of pink in the flowers, shimmers, and the treatment is fluid and animated.[5]

Eleanor included her first two dance-related sketches in the Royal Society of Painter-Etchers and Engravers exhibition of 1950. In the post-war years ballet was both popular and fashionable and dancers such as Margot Fonteyn and Michael Somes were acknowledged stars. In 1950 *The Daily Mirror* featured them and other dancers in a cartoon strip about an imaginary ballet company called 'The Ruggles'. The BBC had its own touring ballet company. In dance Eleanor found a new subject for her interests and she began to haunt Sadler's Wells Theatre and Ballet Rambert both to watch the dancers themselves and to gain access backstage. It was the dancers in preparation, as they applied make-up or rested and waited in the wings, who provided inspiration for her many pencil sketches. She was interested in shape, form, costume, whereas she found on-stage performance less interesting. Eleanor's own finished works were never sentimental: ballet itself is tough.

One Sunday afternoon in November 1951 Eleanor went to the Mercury Theatre in Notting Hill Gate to see a full dress rehearsal by the London Theatre Ballet of *Hoops*, a new ballet by Poulenc about a fantastical circus with choreography by Walter Gore and sets and costumes by Kenneth Rowell. Eleanor was enchanted and wrote to the company to ask if she could meet them. A couple of days later she met two of the dancers and eventually she drew the whole of the company (although Yvonne Cartier was a poor model since she could not sit still or stop talking and Eleanor could not concentrate). They in turn introduced her to their own friends. They were all young people who had came to London from the Empire and beyond in order to educate themselves and in search of a cultural life they could not find back home. Although they had little money they had youth and energy, and they were artistic and open to experience, all qualities which appealed to Eleanor. These new friends whose names filled her diaries included dancers such as Elaine Fifield from Australia, Thalia Karras from South Africa, Yvonne Cartier from New Zealand, Peggy von Praagh and Selena Wylie, and Michael Holmes of the Ballet Rambert; Sérgio Viotti, an actor, director and playwright from Brazil; Peter Brinson, a writer on dance and later a director of the Calouste Gulbenkian Foundation; Pat Fitzgerald, a midwife, and Ted Carr, a composer, who were both from New Zealand.

The Letter
watercolour

Another of the young dancers was 'a beautiful young man' called Kenneth Russell. He lacked the talent to be an outstanding dancer although he could do character roles like Dr Copelius in *Coppélia* with effect. However his secondary interest was photography. He took pictures of some of the *objets d'art* in Eleanor's house, became interested in film-making, and in time went on to become a film director instead.

These friends were mostly twenty years younger than her, for Eleanor by now was over forty, but there seemed to them to be no difference in age. To them she was always young. 6 Hammersmith Terrace became a second home. Thalia Karras, a South African dancer of Greek extraction, had tremendous talent with dramatically beautiful looks but her parents in South Africa kept a restaurant and she loved food. Eleanor made her stay in Hammersmith Terrace where she could be kept on a suitable diet. When they were on tour in the provinces dancers could come back for the night for a bath and wash their clothes, and Mrs Laurie would leave out supper for them. Eleanor could also see what was right or wrong immediately and she gave advice on presentation: because Yvonne Cartier's hair was obviously wrong Eleanor bought her a wig to appear on stage. She was supportive too in other ways. Out of friendship for Ted Carr, in October 1953 she went to the Festival Hall to hear one of his compositions, his *Overture*. Afterwards she said, 'I love Ted, I just wish I felt the same about his music.' In 1954 he won a scholarship to go to Rome but by Christmas he had not received the money for a commission and he was broke. Eleanor invited all his dance and musician friends for a traditional dinner of turkey and Christmas pudding and told them she had a surprise. When they arrived they found Carr. Eleanor had paid for his return air fare and he stayed as her guest for two weeks.

Another member of Eleanor's close circle was the Australian pianist Noel Mewton-Wood who was also a close friend and interpreter of Benjamin Britten. Eleanor had heard him play at the National Gallery in 1943 and now he was living with his partner William Federic at 2 Hillgate Place near Notting Hill Gate tube station – their address was in her diary. In 1953 he was preparing for a concert tour in Germany when Federic fell ill, then died from appendicitis, leaving Mewton-Wood overwhelmed by grief and guilt at not having encouraged Federic to seek medical help earlier. In his despair he threw a glass filled with gin and cyanide at the wall of the music room of his flat and breathed in the fumes, killing himself. 'Noel died aged 31,' Eleanor wrote bleakly in her diary for December 5th. She attended his funeral a week later. In January she listened to a broadcast by Sir Arthur Bliss about the young pianist for whom he had written a piano sonata. Noel's death cast a shadow. Eleanor, although conservative in many ways, was always tolerant of people who led unorthodox lives. In fact she often seemed to prefer their company.

Aside from these new friends she continued to see Robert Austin, and arranged visits to the cinema and the ballet with his wife and daughters. Austin was still in touch with Mollie Bernhard-Smith, his former lover. She was a short, plump woman who wore her hair in 'telephones' on her ears, a fashion long out of date. 'I am glad to hear of you,' he wrote, 'and to

H/C printer's proof

Sara Sproule and Robert Austin in Sara Sproule's garden in Norfolk

know nothing is more amiss than that your hair is white. I hope for my delectation you are still as round as ever. I couldn't bear you to be thin.'[6] He was forced to give up engraving after he began to lose the use of his right thumb which made it impossible for him to hold the burin. 'I am fast becoming a Saturday afternoon painter,'[7] he said, regretting that he did not have enough time. Ada Austin died in 1958. Clare, the elder daughter, left London but Eleanor continued to see her sister Rachel at Lyngard House. Eleanor was always very protective of the family's reputation. A few years before her death Eleanor gave a portfolio of drawings to the RWS for sale, and among the pictures was a sketch of Ada lying nude in a Norfolk reed-bed. By then Ada had been dead for fifty years, the sketch was not titled and no-one other than Eleanor could have identified the model. A few weeks later Eleanor asked for the drawing to be returned and so it was given back to her.

A pretty red-haired young woman called Sara Sproule, who had been one of Austin's students at Ambleside, became part of the Austin household at Lyngard House – even more so perhaps than Eleanor and Ruth had been. Sara was a couple of years younger than Eleanor and in time she too was elected a member of both the Royal Watercolour Society and the Royal Society of Painter-Etchers and Engravers. After the war when the Royal College of Art was back in London Sara became Austin's secretary. Whenever she came into the Schools she was always with him, carrying his bags, and the students, young men just out of the forces, inevitably sniggered as they watched the pair go into Austin's office. Sara had a daughter called Anna who was brought up by Sara's mother. She told everyone that the father had been an officer in the armed forces who had been killed. Later Sara bought her own house a couple of miles from Burnham Overy Staithe, and she and Austin spent their lives together although they never married. Anna only learnt that Robert Austin was her father when she was an adult. Eleanor can never have known that he had fathered Anna: had she done so it would surely only have made matters worse for her. In the later years of his life she no longer saw Austin. When he retired in 1970 as President of the Royal Society of Painter-Etchers and Engravers (although he remained as President of the Royal Watercolour Society) Eleanor preserved the letter circulated among members which recorded the small ceremony, marking the words 'Bob's reply provided a Happy Ending with its characteristic pith, dry humour, sound sense and underlying modesty. A memorable occasion indeed.'

Ballerina
graphite on red-brown paper

In February 1980 the Ashmolean Museum held an exhibition of Robert Austin's work. In its review *The Daily Telegraph* commented:

> Austin was the victim of one of those changes in fashion so common and so complete where the arts are concerned; in his last years before his death in 1973 etching and engraving were out of fashion.[8]

In his last illness Sara dragged his bed out of his bedroom so that he could die in the studio of the chapel at Burnham Overy Staithe amid the air and light from its big windows. It was his last wish. For Austin, Eleanor had been a warm friend. For Eleanor, Robert Austin meant much more. Her greatest love was her greatest disappointment, she told a friend. He was the love of her life: she never met anyone else who mattered and so she never let him go. Perhaps too, she felt that his loss represented what she felt she had missed – a family life with children. For all that she thought Austin had used and disappointed her, she spoke of him as 'remarkable', and she lived surrounded by his pictures which hung on the walls of her houses. In earlier, happier days, she had been forever on the telephone buying yet another of his pictures.

One day one of the dancers told Eleanor about someone called Nesta Brooking who ran a ballet school. Perhaps Eleanor might be interested in sketching there. She gave her the telephone number for the school which Eleanor put into her overall pocket and immediately forgot about. Some weeks later, when about to give her overall to the wash, she found the paper in the pocket and put it into a wastepaper bin. Then she retrieved it again and decided on an impulse to make a phone call. Nesta Brooking answered the telephone and at the end of the conversation she invited Eleanor to meet her at her ballet studio. The meeting with Nesta changed Eleanor's life.

1 Howard Hodgkin, How to be an Artist, *Burlington Magazine*, 7 September 1982

2 EEH memoir

3 EEH to Paige Hudson, 2 March 1955

4 EEH archive.

5 Mary Sorrell, *Art News and Review*, 20 May 1950

6 Robert Austin to Mollie Bernhard-Smith, undated 1958

7 Robert Austin to Mollie Bernhard-Smith, undated 1958

8 *Daily Telegraph*, 18 February 1980

Chapter Five – The Brooking School of Ballet

Nesta Brooking was forty-seven and Eleanor forty-two when in mid-May 1954 they met for the first time. Nesta's own dancing career had ended because of a damaged Achilles tendon. She was a lively and 'feisty' woman, always very demanding, short, with a face surrounded by natural brown curls. As with Eleanor, one never seemed to notice her true age. She was also fiercely ambitious for her work. With a bank loan of £50 she had managed to set up a school in an old school hall on the edge of Primrose Hill by the Regent's Canal. The former kitchen department had been converted into a school room and dressing room, and the main hall was now the studio.

Nesta was born in Manchester in 1906 and brought up outside Chester. Her mother was interested in music and took professional singing lessons, whereas her father, who worked in the rubber industry, had literary interests and was the founder of the Rudyard Kipling Society. When she was only six Nesta began attending dance classes; and in the First World War she was one of a group of little girls who danced and performed little scenes for wounded soldiers. After she left school she determined to pursue a career in dance and moved to London and began to attend classes run by Margaret Craske in West Street. Craske taught the Cecchetti Method which aims to build up essential characteristics of style through rigid training and self-awareness so that pupils become self-reliant rather than imitative dancers. The Method itself was developed by Enrico Cechetti. After dancing with the Imperial Russian Ballet Cechetti had taught individual dancers such as Pavlova and Nijinsky as well as Serge Diaghilev's Ballet Russe Company; Nesta taught the Cecchetti Method in her own school.

Nesta

Her own first employment as a choreographer was on a rather different level. At the suggestion of Margaret Craske she went to work at the Cambridge Theatre for Phyllis Dixey, a beautiful dancer but too tall for classical ballet, who was setting up her own company. Dixey's husband, 'a rather unsavoury man'[1] saw the possibility of using his wife in a striptease act to be done,' said Nesta, 'with taste and daring finesse – 'coquetry beneath a demure appearance!' Between Phyllis Dixey's own acts, which used a lot of fans, dancers gave performances to raise the quality of the Company as a whole. At the time all this was considered artistic.

Subsequently Nesta performed in *The King and I* and toured with the Carl Rosa Opera. After working for three months with Ninette de Valois at Sadlers Wells de Valois asked her to take over her own company at the Abbey Theatre in Dublin, but within a few months this failed because of financial problems. Nesta subsequently founded a small company of her own with Ernest Berk, a Danish dancer and producer. However this ended with Nesta losing – no doubt through naïvety – a great deal of her own money, and she had to sell many of her own possessions in order to avert all-out war with him.

After Eleanor's telephone call Nesta invited her to come to Primrose Hill in order to meet the great dancer Tamara Karsavina who was visiting the studio. In 1910 Karsavina had created Mikhail Fokine's *Firebird* for Diaghilev. She was now sixty-nine but she still had immense presence and it was said of her that she could silence a room just by entering it. Eleanor sat in the gallery to watch Karsavina perform. Afterwards Nesta asked Eleanor if she could see her drawings but Eleanor had to tell her that she had been so enthralled by this elderly lady in leg-warmers somehow transforming herself into the dazzling Firebird that she had not so much as lifted her pencil. Eleanor stayed a week at the school, and on the Friday morning she went to watch the Cecchetti School who were auditioning for the BBC. The two women soon became close friends and began to meet frequently. In August they went to the Cotswolds to stay for a couple of nights, then to Suffolk, soon followed by visits to the theatre to see *I Am a Camera* with Dorothy Tutin, and to the Old Vic to see Michael Holmes in *Macbeth*.

Nesta also found a place for Eleanor in the school: 'Nesta Brooking, a most unusual teacher and personality attracted me to that work of hers for, and with, dedicated students,'[2] Eleanor wrote. Although the school already had staff and in Norman Higgins, a resident composer-pianist, there was an obvious need for an artist to help design the shows and the costumes. This was a role which Eleanor fulfilled, and she brought to it her own natural good taste and experience. It was very hard work, but it was satisfying work. And for Eleanor, the Brooking School of Ballet and General Education gave her access to the young. In her forties and single she would never now have children of her own, but she responded to the energy and imagination of young people and enjoyed their companionship – as they enjoyed hers. Undoubtedly her financial backing was also able to help although a touring ballet she funded for Nesta did not pay its way. Eleanor threw all her energies into the school and her involvement with it lasted some thirty years.

It was through Nesta that Eleanor was introduced to the teachings of George Ivanovitch Gurdjieff. Eleanor was to say that Gurdjieff's teachings were the most important thing in her life and her greatest regret was that she had not encountered them earlier. A photograph of Gurdjieff who had died in 1948 – a great, domed head with a theatrical moustache and dark, compassionate eyes – always hung in her bedroom.

Gurdjieff was born in Armenia, probably in 1866, where his father was an *asokh* or bard. It was a deeply traditional, patriarchal society but at the same time Gurdjieff had exposure to modern knowledge, especially experimental science. However finding answers to the fundamental questions of life neither in religion nor in science he travelled through Asia and the Middle East in search of answers. The search itself, he came to believe, is the principal spiritualising force in human life: a transforming search, rather than a search for transformation. Gurdjieff began his work as a teacher in Moscow in 1912, on the eve of the Russian Revolution; the first Institute for the Harmonious Development of Man was organised in Tbilisi in Georgia in 1919 and subsequently it moved to Fontainebleau-Avon in France. Man, Gurdjieff taught, is an unfinished creation. He is not fully Man, a unique being; he behaves as an automaton who walks through life as in a dream, watching existence happen around him, but he is not truly awake. Much of Gurdjieff's writing seems esoteric and, at first encounter, almost impenetrable, but his fundamental intention was to help rouse man to the meaning of his existence and to the efforts he must make in order to realise significance in the life he has been given. And he must keep on always challenging himself. To this end his adherents set up self-observation groups and centres for his teachings. Nesta met Gurdjieff at his apartment in Paris where he cooked dinner for her and some of his followers. A few small tables had been pushed together to create a small and intense space. After a number of toasts with strong alcohol Gurdjieff asked each of his guests in turn, 'What kind of an idiot are you?' Of course most people had no idea but it represented a kind of existential challenge, both joking and serious, undercutting their certainties so that people let their masks slip. Nesta remembered too that he always carried with him a little bag of sweets in his pocket. To those who looked on him as a spiritual master it was as a kind of provocation: when he met them he offered them a sweet, once again they did not know what to do. In people's reaction something of the real person came through.

Eleanor became part of a Gurdjieff study group led by Jane Heap who had been sent by Gurdjieff to London in 1935. Heap was a short, stocky American woman with short cropped hair who wore masculine clothes. She fizzed with energy. Before her involvement with Gurdjieff she had already made a considerable contribution to twentieth century literature. With her partner Margaret Anderson and Ezra Pound she had edited *The Little Revue*, a magazine which between 1914 and 1929 had published work by some of the most significant writers of the era – transatlantic modernists such as T.S. Eliot, Ernest Hemingway, W.B. Yeats, Gertrude Stein, Marcel Duchamp and Jean Cocteau. (In 1920 the U.S. Post Office seized and burnt four issues of *The Little Review* which included the opening chapters of *Ulysses* on its first publication in America.) In 1925 Heap moved to Paris to study before going to England ten years later. She remained in London throughout the war. Jane Heap's teaching was electrifying. 'You are my work –unless you are working I can't give you what I want to give you,' she challenged her group continually. The interior search was all about attention and self-observation: 'Unless one is connecting with one's emotional centre it is impossible to say I am or I wish to be.' At the same time she was both ferociously eccentric and wonderfully inspired. On one occasion Heap told her group to write an oratorio in a week. Eleanor said the result was dreadful but it was a marvellous education. Work was a spiritual exercise in itself and all of these experiences offered food for thought and spiritual growth.

Another area of activity was at Bray in Berkshire where members were encouraged to take part in art or craft or science. An old chicken farm had been turned into workshops for painting, tapestry work, collage, and making puppets and toys – even an old-fashioned gipsy caravan was made there. Out of this Jane Heap had the idea of opening an antique shop in St John's Wood High Street to sell neglected and forgotten old toys which could be retrieved from attics and lumber rooms. The shop she set up was called after its speciality, The Rocking Horse. When it first started the horses were first put out for sale in the state in which they had been found but then it was decided that it would be better if they were sold fully restored. And so Eleanor and the other workers at Bray enthusiastically repainted the horses, repairing and replacing all the harnesses, rosettes, studs and the bits for the mouths. The very first horse sold for £40 which seemed an enormous sum and before long the shop had a stable-full. Eleanor also did the artwork for The Rocking Horse, drawing small flyers with designs of horses, or larger ones of a sort of universal atelier of horses, antique dolls, teapots, china and prams. After Jane Heap died in 1964 the shop lasted for only a short while longer. On New Year's Day 1965 Eleanor wrote to Paige, 'The 6 weeks before Christmas is always hard work for me in our workroom to the shop, so many orders to finish in time,'[3] but it closed soon afterwards.

Eleanor's involvement with Nesta and the school into which she now threw all her energies, as well as The Rocking Horse and the Gurdjieff meetings, inevitably brought new people into her life and separation from her past. There was less time to spend on her own work and so Eleanor exhibited less. In 1955 she had no pictures at all in either of the Royal Watercolour Society exhibitions, and only one the following year. In Spring 1957 her sole picture, 'Meditation on Spring' was sold at the private view to Nesta for £31 10s (a comparatively high price), who also bought pictures by Robert Austin and Philip Connard, a Richmond artist. The RWS Autumn show in 1958 was the Society's 250th exhibition and *The Evening Standard* published a photograph of Rachel and Clare Austin looking at Eleanor's picture 'Dancers in a Studio'. Just two years later Eleanor resigned from both the Royal Watercolour Society and the Royal Society of Painter-Etchers and Engravers. It was as if she was following one of Jane Heap's own aphorisms, 'Do not sit in the same place too long', and was making a clean break from her past as Heap herself had done. This new challenge for herself, sometimes involving a sixteen-hour day, she saw as nourishment for the Gurdjieff movement. Eleanor carried on sketching for the rest of her life but out of typical modesty she did not regard any of her work as worth keeping and it was forty years before she exhibited again.

By now the Brooking School had moved to two storeys in a former piano factory at 110 Marylebone High Street. Next door there was a jeweller's shop and on the opposite side of the road a Wimpy Bar. The school provided space for two studios, changing rooms, offices and classrooms, and even a small kitchen. The studio was on the top storey of the building and a new sprung floor suitable for dancing was laid over the old wooden one. On three sides of the

Rocking Horse flyer

AT THE ROCKING HORSE

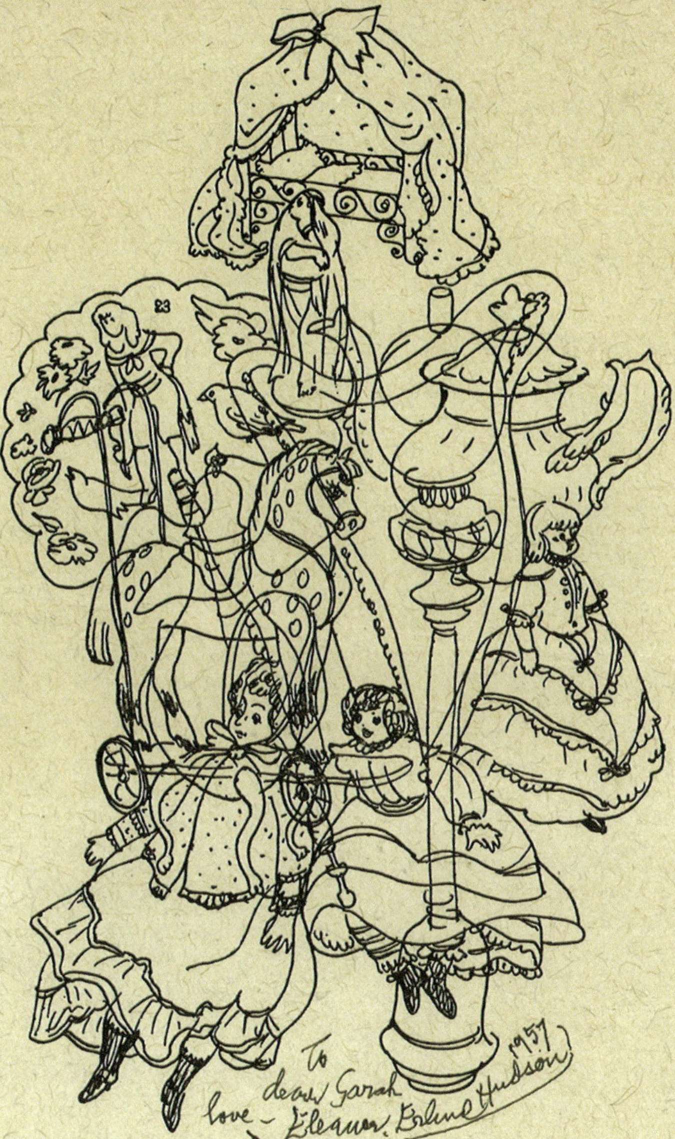

23 st johns wood high street nw8

pri 6681

studio there were views across the roofs of the London skylines. Nesta fed the pigeons from the windows. In one corner there was an alcove where Norman Higgins played the piano and where Nesta took sips of her favourite reviving concoction of whisky, liquorice and hot water. A door led outside to a steep, rather precarious – and not altogether safe – fire-escape.

In its prospectus the Brooking School advertised 'a balanced education' in ballet and related subjects for a career on the stage, in choreography or in teaching. In addition to the daily ballet class there were lessons in the Cecchetti syllabus, *pas de deux*, repertoire, character, historical and modern dance, as well as in art and drama. Training was also given in the art of make-up and the making and care of costumes. Ballet is a hard discipline and Nesta had a very high expectation both of herself and of others. Her pupils had to learn to be more than just dancers but artists as well, always aware and thinking of what they were doing. There was no room for stars. When children came into the studio they had to walk around the walls not across the centre of the room, and they were not to interrupt. At social functions they were taught how to entertain and mingle in order to learn social skills. They had to observe etiquette and be neat and tidy in all things. And so the boys had to sweep the floors and the girls wash them with boiling water (detergent was not allowed); everything was done rhythmically as if in a ritual dance. Every day the girls – not the boys who to the girls' annoyance were

free from the duty – had to prepare the frugal lunch of bird-like portions of Wensleydale or Caerphilly cheese, sticks of celery with their strings removed, and hexagonal-shaped biscuits. Unsurprisingly the teachers, who sat together at one end of the room, generally found reasons to bring in their own meals.

The children were in awe in of Nesta. When she entered the studio, they fell silent – the children did not dare do otherwise. She had her eccentricities. She could not remember girls' names so she called them all Susan. When a girl objected, Nesta said, 'Well, all right, Susan, from now on you'll be called Olga'. And she could be brutal. A girl appeared with a fringe after Nesta had told her not to so she took a pair of scissors, walked over to her and chopped it off. Everything was a cause for drama, nothing was incidental. Writing about Nesta after her friend's death, Eleanor evoked the atmosphere of the Brooking School:

> In a tough seven day week, she also came to understand values, say: r***elaxation***. Disastrous work interference or perhaps even maddening Ballet-mums! So, off to the junior students' Little House [where younger pupils boarded] with a pair of shears to cut the huge thorny hedge till anger and tension were worked out because the moaning of a victim had no place, ever.
> And let's talk of GUTS. Perhaps crashes in the street, the odd shirker student spreads the news, "Miss Brooking's in hospital; we can meander in late." HORRORS! The Studio Class is in full swing but a puzzled teacher stops it; "Why are all your right arms stuck out like that?" "Well, Miss Brooking, that's how you're demonstrating!" "Can't you see that's only splints and plaster?" as she peers through a black eye and bandages! Or, what about this motto? "Take hold strongly, let go lightly!" And that lightening of touch when things got too solid, the use of fun to keep judgment and balance, by laughter.[4]

But sometimes even Eleanor would say quietly in the midst of a great commotion, 'Nesta, do you have to?'

Eleanor worked downstairs but came in and out, standing at the back of the class to watch. She had her own quiet presence and she brought common sense. Eleanor thought of herself as a professional-minded amateur. She was fun and creative, happy to help the students. A pupil ordered out of the studio by Nesta could find refuge with her; Eleanor would look up, say nothing, and hand her a piece of sewing. While she did not teach art – and never spoke of her career as an artist – she taught costume-making as well as simple skills to the boys such as button-sewing. Everything was given her meticulous dedication. She bought bales of spoilt goods in the East End for very little money to use as material for the shows the school staged at Christmas, and dyed them in bright colours. Half of Eleanor's life seemed to be spent at work on her little Swiss sewing machine.

Studio, Brooking School of Ballet
(Eleanor fourth from left, Nesta second from right),
Marylebone High Street

Nesta and she led demanding lives. There was little time to go home during the day so they kept beds in their office where they rested before evening classes. Eleanor's health was always a concern. During the Suez Crisis of 1956 her doctor in Harley Street ensured that she receive additional petrol coupons so that she could use her car at all times. She could never bear to be in the company of anyone who smoked, and she still suffered from palpitations of the heart as well as from a bad throat and breathing problems. If she suffered an attack at school someone would be sent out to Ainsworth's, a local druggist's shop for medication. On Friday afternoons Nesta and she regularly went to Cockfosters for an appointment with Dr Vickerey who had a homeopathic practice.

Despite its many idiosyncrasies the Brooking School had a high reputation but it was self-contained and did not go along with much of the ballet world. Mary Clarke, the editor of the *The Dancing Times,* wrote an article about an evening choreographic class:

> A typical evening this term has consisted of exercises of various kinds and then small choreographic fragments devised by the students to incorporate the basic shape or "weight" of the exercise. Group works are also done by the students and in every case Miss Brooking and all the fellow students discuss and analyse the work in progress. Norman Higgins provides the music, plays for the classes, and gives the boys and girls advice on a suitable choice of music if they wish to work from existing scores.... as the term progresses, careful notes are kept of each evening session so that there is a record of the ground covered. Some students from the Brooking School attend and make themselves available as "bodies" for the young choreographers, but nearly all soon get involved in the excitement of the creation. Often, when a group work which has been devised by the students, working alone in the smaller studio, is brought up to the big studio for inspection, a few pertinent suggestions from Miss Brooking or the onlookers will give the young choreographer the clue to solving a difficult or unsatisfactory section.[5]

Described by a friend 'as the sort of person who could be resourceful with felt and coat-hangers', Eleanor also designed the scenery for the Christmas shows. A hundred and fifty people crowded into the studio which had been turned into a theatre for the night. Her Victorian screen covered with cut-outs always stood on the stage. The shows, which always included new ideas, new music by Norman Higgins, and new choreography, were well thought of in the ballet world and they were reviewed in the national press as some of the best of their kind in London. One of the great supporters of the school was Cyril Beaumont, a tall, thin, rather old-fashioned Edwardian gentleman who had been a great friend of Enrico Cecchetti himself. Together they had documented Cecchetti's Method. Beaumont's shop at 75 Charing Cross Road was filled with a cornucopia of dance memorabilia. It was part of the ethos of the school that pupils should have a general education – a pupil who felt too unwell to dance would be sent to visit the Wallace Museum a few streets away. To help encourage their education, each year Beaumont judged an essay competition in which students were allowed to write on whatever subject they chose, and he presented a prize. After his death his former assistant Jill Ann Bowden and her sister Nancy continued this tradition. There were other kindnesses too. One Christmas a £100 cheque arrived anonymously at the home of a needy pupil. It can only have come from Eleanor. When the same pupil had a problem with his Achilles tendon he was taken for treatment without any fuss, and everything was paid for. Indeed the two women would willingly help anyone who came through the door, whether or not he or she had money, out of generosity. By the end of their school years pupils had been given a good education. If they had talent they went on to another school and a career in dance or, if this was not realistic, to other good jobs or occupations.

Eleanor and Jessamy Pollock in costume for BBC ballet King's Cross!

At the time when Eleanor and Nesta first met, Nesta was renting a room at 65 Carlton Hill in St John's Wood. The house belonged to a member of Jane Heap's group called Michael Currer Briggs who had significant private means. When he asked Heap how he might best use his money for the good of the Gurdjieff Society she suggested to him that he could help by buying a house to share with other members. As a result he bought the Carlton Hill property and, subsequently, 2 Abbey Gardens. Currer Briggs worked in television as a director and a producer; he was Associate Producer on Peter Brook's 1978 film of Gurdjieff's *Meetings with Remarkable Men*. The third member of the household was Marjorie Bayes who worked in the Society's office; she was a Quaker and a reserved, rather prim woman. Apart from their interest in Gurdjieff, the three did not necessarily have much in common but they got on well with one another.

Shortly before Christmas 1959 Eleanor was attacked outside her house in Hammersmith Terrace and had her handbag snatched (it contained the stamps she had just bought for her Christmas cards). She was concussed and had to spend a couple of days in hospital but it only made her more determined to continue in the life she had chosen for herself. At the same time she felt she needed a retreat where she could get away from the stresses of London. Robert Austin knew that Molly Bernhard-Smith wanted to sell Thatched Cottage, her cottage in the village of St Nicholas-at-Wade near Birchington in Kent and he thought it might interest Eleanor. Nesta and she decided to buy it together for £3200. Austin wrote to Molly:

My Dear, I fancy those two girls would want to buy your cottage at St Nicholas! That last visit I think has done it!... How all this might be effected I can't quite at this moment think. But it would seem that the situation should be handled carefully & it would come off. One item which might easily be done to help is that one or two things could be bought in with the cottage - bed, chest of drawers... I could see that an amount of thought has gone into the whole question and I doubt if you will get a better price from these girls than anyone else to acquiesce in these modest ideas.

Eleanor and neice Myrth

Perhaps Austin now saw Eleanor and Nesta, 'these two girls', in much the same light as he had seen Eleanor and Ruth twenty years or so earlier.

Molly took Austin's advice and she sold the cottage, leaving furniture and much else behind. It seemed as if nothing had ever been thrown away and old coats and mackintoshes hung from nails in the oak beams about the main room. Nesta and Eleanor took over Thatched Cottage, which had been built from dark pink brick in the fifteenth century and was now covered in ivy, and they cleaned, 'de-cobwebbed' and emptied it. Molly herself used to return to sit with her old hat and sunshade in the garden which Austin had enjoyed in the 'altogether'. When a great friend, Diana Barker, a Cecchetti teacher, visited they went into Birchington to buy ladies' bicycles. St Nicholas was only a couple of miles inland from the sea. (Whenever he came to stay Molly Bernhard-Smith always insisted that the sculptor Jacob Epstein go down and bathe because he smelt.)

> After trying them [the bicycles] we said Right! We take the lot! SOLD OUT go. What amazement! So three ladies rode the rutted lanes and over the railway and the DUNES to the breakers of the North Sea - FREEDOM![6]

For seventeen years Thatched Cottage was part of Eleanor's life. Eleanor wrote to Susan and Paige who were about to move to Jersey:

> Here I am in the country, in the day it has turned bitterly cold, which is a pity as my still sore chest doesn't like it, but inside, the cottage is very warm & snug up & down, and our two old dears in the next cottage (Mrs and Mrs Gambrill, old Kent farming couple) keep it aired in general & warmed up in particular when one is due to arrive. So actually one puts weary legs out of the car, opens the welcoming unlocked cottage door & comes in to a glorious red coal & wood fire, a nice crackling boiler in the kitchen & a laid tray of teacups, with kettle singing on the hob. Long may this lovely thing last, but oh my dear! All my favourite people are moving into their eighties, bar a few whose job & pleasure is not to coddle me but only themselves. Each time I give thanks for the sweet friendly old timers who are at ease with one completely from a so-called different social scale, who love a friendly chat & take an interest in what tree branches must ***not*** be cut because they twine so picturesquely - and who really enjoy making the brass shine & bottling the plums... Of course I and friends come here in the winter now, a custom almost to spend New Year's Eve here under the glorious country sky instead of noisy London... Here we are snug as a bug when snowbound under the thatch & cosily sheltered inside our rambling orchard - while beyond, the miles of open land, cornfields mainly, undulate under the brilliant winter stars to the sea on two sides. We are in the Isle of Thanet and I suppose the sea & the smell of air from all the lands of Siberia makes this wonderful crisp air that puts new life into one...[7]

As the unconventionalities of Eleanor's life increased so she kept herself more and more to herself and apart from her family. She spoke little to them about her life in art. Although she always genuinely wanted to know what her 'father's progeny' were doing she was reluctant to involve them in her own activities. She was busy and did not think they might be interested. They were rarely invited to the school concerts although those who lived in London would gladly have gone. The Gurdjieff Society was never spoken about at all. Eleanor was instinctively secretive anyway and perhaps a hangover from the habits of wartime together with an almost Victorian personal discretion only increased her reticence. Without explaining why he might want to, Nesta and Eleanor nagged Norman Higgins to visit a retired diplomat called Miss Brenda Tripp. Eventually, worn down by their insistence, he went to see her and found that she seemed to talk sense: Miss

Tripp was a member of the Gurdjieff Society which Higgins subsequently also joined. Even many years later when her great nephew Stephen Hudson showed an interest in Gurdjieff – something which delighted Eleanor – there was unspoken agreement between them that their involvement was not to be discussed within the rest of the family.

Eleanor was absent-minded. Her eldest brother Edmund wrote crossly early in 1962:

> I was more than thankful to see your writing and your letter to Bodil. If it had not come I would have been forced to write to find out whether you were ill, and if not I would have been contemplating the need to write in some sorrow and some anger. After all, a third year running with no acknowledgement of a Christmas gift would have been a bit hard to bear. I'm glad it has not after all arisen. Also I was aware of having sent you a letter which was neither peremptory or demanding and yet which on the very simplest and elementary consideration of courtesy did require an answer on your part, an answer never came. The only way I can work the poison out of my system is to disclose it in this way. I'm glad you liked the slippers. I was with Bodil when we chose them. We had to pay the bill in due course, without any certainty that the goods had safely arrived.[8]

Hopeless at time-keeping, she was invariably late even for weddings. When one of her nephews married, his new wife found her first encounter with Eleanor deeply alarming. Eleanor seemed to her a Frida Kahlo figure with her Bohemian, gipsy clothing and her strong, uncompromising opinions. But others of that generation found her oddities endearing. They were what made Eleanor such a much-loved aunt. Close friends from the worlds of Gurdjieff and ballet, her family and other areas of Eleanor's life were often quite unaware of one another's existence. It was as if this was how she kept the plates spinning, and everything alive within her.

1 Nesta Brooking memoir

2 EEH memoir

3 EEH to Paige and Susan Hudson, 1 January 1965

4 Funeral eulogy

5 *The Dancing Times*, December 1974

6 EEH memoir

7 EEH to Paige and Susan Hudson, 28 December 1969

8 Edmund Hudson to EEH, 8 February 1962

Chapter Six – Bosham

In 1970 Eleanor and Nesta bought another cottage. On Thursday evenings after work they had been in the habit of going to a coffee shop in St John's Wood and had got to know the owner, Mrs Penry Jones. She told them about the fisherman's cottage she owned at Old Bosham, a little fishing village in West Sussex near Chichester, and she offered them the cottage for a weekend stay. Not long afterwards she told Eleanor and Nesta that she was moving away and that the cottage was for sale. They decided almost instantly that they would buy it from her, for £1100 each, and so Number 2, New Buildings along with its contents – old brasses, chests of drawers and furniture – became theirs. Like Thatched Cottage, the two hundred year old, pink brick cottage was quaint and pretty. A cupboard door opened to reveal a flight of steep winding stairs, and from the bottom step one could put one's hand onto the first floor. From outside the climbing roses pushed at the upstairs window.

The oldest buildings in Bosham were clustered around the harbour. According to village legend this was where King Canute commanded the waves to turn back. Eleanor used to send her visitors to see Bosham's Saxon church. On one wall hung a copy of a scene in the Bayeux Tapestry which showed Harold meeting King Edward the Confessor before deciding with William of Normandy who would inherit the throne of England. Bosham's history interested Eleanor but, more than that, the village was a place which fulfilled her intense need and appreciation of the natural world. In front of her cottage lay the sea:

> Miles of water, moving tide by tide, high or neap tides as still as a shining mirror looking glass, or whipped into a frenzy of waves and spray flung over the cottage's "Trippet" sea wall. Huge skies flaunting blazing stars, Orion with his belt of 3 or the fixed earthly point of the guiding North Star - Ursa Major circulating around it day and night, weekly, monthly, yearly, as seasons change. Or else the snow white giant clouds, piled up range above range into the bluest azure of the high and wide space.[1]

Together Eleanor and Nesta gathered bleached white flotsam from the beach to burn in the fire grate. The salt gave off emerald and blue flickers amidst the red and orange flames.

A few years after they bought 2 New Buildings the last building plot on the Trippet came up for sale; Eleanor went to a public auction and bid for the old hay meadow in order that she could build a house of her own and protect the rest of the field from speculators. For an architect she employed a friend called Wendy Harris, a fellow member of the Gurdjieff Society where she taught dance. Harris's previous work had mostly been in creating new schools for post-war planning developments but at Meadow House she blended the traditional with the modern; it was Eleanor's intention to construct a house and a garden which would fit appropriately into the end of Old Bosham village 'without shock or undue inappropriate style or formality'. Outside the architecture was traditional and a firm of builders from Chichester was employed to build a clapboard and pink brick 'complete real house'. Eleanor kept changing her mind over details but in its lightness and simplicity it seemed to reflect both her New England and her Scandinavian backgrounds. Inside, the house was cool, spacious and contemporary with big windows and white walls; the large sitting room became an excellent room for entertaining and for music-making – there was both an upright and a small ship's piano; and she hung paintings by her Hammersmith neighbour Mary Fedden. As Meadow House went up in 1976, during a summer which never seemed to end, so, to everyone's surprise, the unploughed field bloomed with turnip flowers. Typically, Eleanor made friends with her neighbours, Vera and Syd Fossey, who came to work for her. Vera looked after the house while Syd tended the garden which was transformed from a field into lawns and flowers and vegetable beds. In the greenhouse Eleanor planted a vine which produced the white muscat grapes she had known in her Devon childhood.

Eleanor was now told by her accountant that, as the owner of four houses, she had too much property, and in the event of her death her estate would be liable to a considerable amount of tax. As ever, she trusted her professional adviser and with great generosity she gave Thatched Cottage to Virginia, her niece. Virginia was living in Spain with her husband but she wished to return to England for her children's education. Eleanor also made over her share of 2 New Buildings to Nesta who rented the cottage to Bill and Barry, two friends who worked in the theatre in London.

Visitors were made welcome at Meadow House, as at all Eleanor's other houses. In the autumn of 1979 she lent the house to her nephew Hugh who was between jobs and without a house of his own after having worked abroad for many years. He and his wife and two young children moved in and stayed until the following summer, the children attending the village school. And then in 1994 Eleanor was contacted by an artist and craftsman who had been seriously ill for many months from food-poisoning. Eleanor did not know him but a mutual acquaintance told him go to Bosham if he was to have any chance of recovery. He arrived at Meadow House - with little more than his dog and a change of socks – to find Eleanor sitting at the threshold of her house like an inscrutable figure in some Scandinavian saga. Having listened to his tale and seeing his need to convalesce she took him in, giving him the nursery in which to sleep and work (he was writing a book on medieval contemplatives). For three months he lived at Bosham and became part of the household. When Eleanor and Nesta were at home he witnessed what seemed to him as he put it, the 'choreography' by which they moved about the house, coming together to talk and then parting from one another. Sometimes when they were back in London and he was by himself he lay in the garden swaddled in blankets – a neighbour, a judge's wife, called the police because she thought he must be a vagrant. After his eventual recovery he wrote to Nesta: 'I can see you conversing with the plants in the garden... I lingered too over your description of Eleanor, "always dressed", ceaselessly working to keep life moving.' He observed of Eleanor how, in the words of St Thierry, one part of her was always kept private and hidden to herself. *Secretum meum mihi*.[2]

Eleanor and Nesta in the garden at Meadow House

The journey back and forth from London to Bosham through the green Sussex lanes became a tremendous pleasure in itself but it was all Eleanor wanted and she had little desire to go further. The prospect of any journey involving travel on water – she suffered from sea-sickness – filled her with horror. Nesta and she were forever packing for Bosham, preparing hampers to fill the boot and the back seat. It was just like the old days of charabancs and Hudson family outings to Dartmoor or to Slapton Sands for picnics on the beach. They were prepared for all eventualities. Eleanor once drove into the back of the car in front of her; following her first instincts, she immediately got out of her own car, retrieved the First Aid kit from the boot, and handed out arnica tablets for shock to everyone. Over the years however her constant back pain meant that getting in and out of a vehicle began to be more of a problem and her driving less confident. A neighbour in Hammersmith Terrace once went to help Nesta and Eleanor fasten their seat belts only for them to refuse. Nesta told him, 'Oh no, we never use those. If we're stopped by the police we'll just tell them we're not going far and only live down the road.' He watched as the car juddered away from the kerb, and across the road, weaving from side to side until out of sight. Eleanor finally gave up driving when she put her foot on what she maintained firmly was the brake pedal and the car accelerated. She took this as a warning.

The lease on the Brooking School's Marylebone High Street premises ended in 1987 and the school was forced to close: after nearly forty years the Brooking School of Ballet and General Education was over. Although now 80, Nesta opened another school solely for older children in the parish church hall in Wyndham Place nearby and fitted it out with bars and mirrors. Although she had a few new ideas, after a couple of years this too closed. The heart had gone out of the work. Finally she taught for two lessons a week in a studio in Bond Street. Unlike her own teacher Margaret Craske who, she said, was still teaching when she was 96, Nesta was no longer able to go on. In a fit of crossness she threw away all the films of the dances which had been made at the School over the course of her career. For all that the Brooking School was small many of its former students went on to successful careers in the world of ballet. In the early 1970s she had an exceptional group of six girls whom Nesta referred to as *Les Six* – Kim Petts, Norma Atallah, Kate Woolcombe, Rosemary Horton, Leri O'Gorman and Berenice Waldron – in whom she took exceptional pride. They invariably danced together and Nesta used them to demonstrate, and impress, visitors. But *prima inter pares* among her other students was a South African girl called Monica Mason who first started when the school was still at Primrose Hill. Subsequently she moved on to the Royal Ballet School and eventually she became the Royal Ballet's principal dancer; from 2002 to 2012 she was Director of the Royal School of Ballet itself.

Michael Currer-Briggs, the owner of Nesta's house in Swiss Cottage, died in 1980. He was buried next to Jane Heap in Marylebone Cemetery in a patch of ground where space for four graves – Jane Heap, Currer-Briggs, Marjorie Bayes and Nesta – had been reserved. Subsequently Marjorie and Nesta bought a house in Camden Street off Kensington Church Street. 81 Camden Street was a pretty, three-storey terrace house with a small backyard which would originally have been built for a workman. Nesta and Marjorie lived there together until Marjorie went into a nursing home where she died in 1993.

Eleanor and Nesta, having spent so much of their lives together, now agreed to live with one another and so Eleanor moved into Camden Street. She kept Hammersmith Terrace however and had a housekeeper living there, and, as always, her guests were welcome to stay. If ever Eleanor went back and noticed that just an ornament had been moved she carefully adjusted it to its correct place – such was Eleanor's feeling for the appropriateness of things. In their new lives Nesta did most of the cooking and caring. Neither complained but matters became difficult, necessitating help and re-arranging rooms at Camden Street. 'So glad to have received so much,' Nesta wrote. 'I feel imprisoned here. Glad to help E but she does suffer – to get up and downstairs with a stick and my hand is a long job & she sits or rests – good friends, good talk – but nobody knows the agony and effort.'[3] Eventually they employed carers to look after them both, the last of whom was Ellen Garcia, 'my wonder woman of the Philippines', as Eleanor called her, who stayed for thirteen years from 1998 onwards. Ellen's name was actually Eleanor but she abbreviated it to avoid inevitable confusion. With two strong-minded, independent people confined into a small space the relationship between Nesta and Eleanor was not always easy. Sometimes they had arguments and did not speak to one another for a couple of days but, as well as their mutual need, they were always held together by devotion and respect. They also shared some common values and opinions – such as a fear that if the Labour Party came to power it might abolish the monarchy. Eleanor's politics were conservative but patrician. She did not approve of the sale of council houses, the policy of the incoming Conservative governments of the 1980s, because she considered that that would mean fewer houses for working people to live in. When Stephen her great nephew took part in the Anti-Poll Tax riots of 1990 and was attacked by policemen on horses wielding batons he retreated, badly shaken, to take refuge in Camden Street. Nesta was wholly unsympathetic and merely said, 'A good thing too!' Eleanor offered him a whisky.

Although her name still appeared in the Honorary Retired Members columns of the Royal Watercolour Society and the Royal Society of Painter-Printmakers (as the Painter-Etchers and Engravers were now called) Eleanor no longer had any connection with the art world. Occasionally dealers wrote to her wanting to see her works but she had not updated her entries in reference books for many years. *Who's Who*, in which her name appeared for over sixty years, enquired as to whether or not she was still alive. In 1983 the Imperial War Museum tracked her down and made a tape recording of Eleanor in conversation in which she talked about her life and her wartime experiences. Although she was always happy to tell people her stories – and she remained particularly pleased with her War Museum work – she made no attempt to promote her pictures, and she feared that after her death everything would just end up in a saleroom, be sold for next to nothing and disappear.

Then in 1999 the Spring Exhibition of the Royal Watercolour Society included a number of Eleanor's sketches and drawings at the Society's new home, Bankside Gallery, in order to celebrate the sixtieth anniversary of her election to the Society. It was the first time her pictures had been on show for nearly forty years. Even on this occasion they were not intended for sale but, to her surprise, a visitor asked if he could buy an un-mounted sketch exhibited inside one of the glass cabinets. She was delighted to accept an offer. For a few years afterwards she entered for sale – and sold – yet more of her pictures. She also asked the printmaker and print historian Anthony Dyson to take some new prints from the plates she had made in the 1930s and 1940s. When she received him for the first time she was sitting in her bedroom and he could not help but notice then and always her 'unfailing elegance' even when she was in her dressing gown. He remarked too on the precision of her diction: when Eleanor talked it seemed as if one became aware not just of the words but even the punctuation. 'Once you're over ninety people begin to listen to you,' she remarked to him. It was through Tony Dyson that the British Museum Print Room acquired a number of examples of her work.

Eleanor was often confined to her bedroom. Once when she was there for a few weeks Nesta bought her a set of watercolour paints. Although her hands were arthritic she sat up in bed painting and made a number of small drawings of flowers.[4] Sometimes the flowers were arranged in a white jug in order to show the contrast with the colour as Robert Austin always did in his flower pictures. She showed her watercolours – which were priced cheaply at £100 each – and her etchings in a small exhibition at the Gurdjieff Society's Clarendon Cross Galleries in Holland Park. It was a joint exhibition shared with Trata Maria Dresche, a mosaic-maker, and Verena Keable, who made screen-prints on fabric. Hating fuss, neither Eleanor nor Nesta came to the private view.

On February 1st 2007 *The Daily Mail* printed a double-page spread about three artists, Erlund Hudson, Malvina Cheek and Phyllis Dimond, who were all in their nineties. A couple of weeks later on February 18th all three were invited to a tea party to celebrate Eleanor's 95th birthday at the Imperial War Museum. Eleanor's pictures were brought out of storage for her to look at for the first time in many years, and the artists' conversation was broadcast on the BBC's *Woman's Hour*. For the occasion Eleanor presented the Museum with another drawing entitled 'Comforting the Orphan', a picture of a woman holding a child in her arms. Shortly afterwards the Museum bought a further picture entitled 'Forces Canteen' of men in greatcoats sitting in the canteen drinking tea. It complemented the picture of women at work in a kitchen purchased sixty years earlier. The Wellcome Library also bought a drawing of women cutting up sheets for bandages. Eleanor was delighted and surprised by such very late recognition of her work. Self-effacing by nature she wondered that it should have come to her all, and yet she said that it had come too late. Had it come earlier it would have meant far more. And it also made her question whether abandoning her career in art completely had been too drastic a decision.

On her 62nd birthday, Edmund wrote to Eleanor telling her that he had found a box of old letters in the attic, some of which were from her:

> 50 years, 1 month and 2 days ago you asked me to remember to write to you every week. Maybe I haven't always remembered in the intervening half century, but I hope I haven't been too bad a correspondent. Here is the evidence - enclosed along with much else - of that request.[5]

Edmund's married life had been spent in industry, at ICI and its subsidiary, Scottish Agricultural Industries. His scientific interest had been in the role of fertilizers as an aid in mitigating the problems of hunger and bettering the lives of humanity. A member of the Royal Society of Edinburgh and an Honorary D.Sc. of Heriott-Watt University, he was knighted in 1963. He kept in contact with his mother's Olsen family in the USA and he also read *The New Yorker* weekly, it was an American connection. He died from cancer in 1978 at the age of 75 forty years after the death of his brother Merivale. Every year he had planted out the pink and yellow dahlias which his brother had grown in Norfolk (one of them was called 'Joan Hudson'), then dug them up again carefully from his cold Edinburgh garden for replanting the following spring.

Subsequently Eleanor made Alan, Edmund's eldest son, executor to her will, and for the last twenty-five years of her life she sought his assistance as a go-between with her various professional advisers and in her property affairs.

Elizabeth, the oldest of the brothers and sisters, died in December 1993. Laurence wrote to her daughter about his memories: 'we younger brothers were no doubt a trial to her ... how she appreciated artistic things but basically she was practical and jolly efficient, dealing with domestic chores and finance (including that bug-bear, tax) most ably.' Although Eleanor had seen less of Elizabeth than of any of her brothers, at the end of her own life it was Elizabeth and Helen her mother she wanted, as she must have done when she was a child, during the long, restless hours in the middle of the night when she could not sleep. Paige, Eleanor said, had a special place in her heart. After Susan's recovery she and Paige moved to Kirby Muxloe, another Leicestershire parish, with Paige as vicar-in-charge, but this did not last. After a spiritual crisis he left the ministry. For some years afterwards he ran the Stroud Festival in Gloucestershire, a happy and successful time in his life. He retired to Jersey where Susan and he swam every day in the sea. Caring deeply for his family history he researched and compiled historic family trees; hundreds of letters were inserted into individual envelopes and details about each of them were typed onto the front of the envelope. He died in May 1998 aged 93. Laurence died three years later. Nearly seventy years earlier he had written to Eleanor that 'day by day I am finding more and more pleasure in music. It is more and more one of my great passions.' Music became his whole life. After a career in teaching, he moved in 1951 to Cheltenham where he conducted his own string orchestra, and noted choral societies and served on the committees of many musical organisations including the Cheltenham International Festival. In his mid-40s Laurence qualified as a private pilot and flew solo to the Mediterranean.

Nesta's mental state began to decline. She grew more cantankerous and unreasonable, as well as more possessive of Eleanor, and people she did not know well, which included members of Eleanor's own family, were shoo-ed out of the house with threats to call the police. However all her years of ballet training meant that physically she remained very fit and very erect. If she was unwatched sometimes she walked out of the front door into the street in her night dress at considerable speed and had to be pursued by Ellen and the other carers. Eleanor's bedroom became her office space for writing, receiving visitors and making telephone calls. Inevitably for her this was an immensely trying and distressing time which imposed on her more responsibility when she had less strength and little inclination to deal with necessary paperwork. Yet more than anything she felt the need to hang on and survive Nesta for without her Nesta's life would have been even more bewildered. Eleanor always gave encouragement and if visitors arrived she tried to include Nesta in the conversation. There were times when Nesta would come round and see how irrational her behaviour was, and she would smile amused at herself. In January 2006 when her

Eleanor, Laurence, Paige, Edmund, Elizabeth, June 1976

Nesta,
March 2006
graphite

voice was almost gone, she managed to sit up in bed propped by pillows and let Eleanor sketch her. Most of the drawings turned out as caricatures but a few were successful: a lined and weary face nearly at the end of its life.

Nesta died in March 2006. She was 99. As residents of Bosham, Eleanor and she had been entitled to ask to be buried in the graveyard of Bosham parish church. However when some years previously they approached the vicar of Bosham and mentioned that they were members of the Gurdjieff Society, they had been told that a churchyard burial was impossible. As far as he was concerned followers of Gurdjieff were believers in a cult and he wanted nothing to do with them so instead Nesta was buried at Marylebone Cemetery as had been planned. At the funeral service Eleanor's nephew Hugh read out the eulogy Eleanor had written for her:

> Because it is customary, one of us close in life to this dear life lady, is asked to pay a tribute to her whilst us here, physically, for the last time, and so... Eleanor tries her best... What a nerve! As if it is some kind of human CRUFT'S show! If so, this tribute is a beautiful ROSETTE, full of wonderful little stars so full, that one wonders where to begin, twinkling, not blindingly, but let's say ***endearingly***. I believe that most of us here today, are here because of those very human qualities, mixed up with our Nesta and Quality is the word, with a Capital letter for that has been her life-long search, conducted with unstinting efforts and shared, if found, with generosity and love.
>
> As Jill-Anne Bowden has just told us, about Nesta's work with students, she would risk all of what is called popularity, to help them ***and*** to find the discipline that it is necessary for the Work of CAREER and especially of LIFE. And so the essential opposites, good and bad, of a human being would be allowed to show with openness the tinder-spark to set things moving; and if a knot of old friends gathered and spoke of her, a gale of laughter might burst out at a mention of her name. Oh Nesta, the ***DEVIL***! With their late understanding and affection! Never could the word DULL be associated or linked with the name off NESTA BROOKING...
>
> And for me, Eleanor, her ***Courage!!*** A wonder, to hold and be held with her hands as the moment brought freedom to her Spirit.
>
> Maybe the lifetime's search for truth brought the peace and that real beauty into her face.
>
> Grief is there but we give thanks and a tribute, indeed.

'Her bird has now flown,' wrote Ross Fuller to Eleanor. 'God bless her twinkling feet.' After Nesta's death her bed was kept as it had always been and its continuing presence brought Elea-

Eleanor at Bankside Gallery

nor some comfort. She received a bagful of cards and letters from former students who during their time had complained about Nesta ('who didn't?') but in their own words they all said that Nesta had changed their outlook on life. In following years on Nesta's birthday – which fell on October the thirty-first, Halloween – Ellen drove Eleanor and Nesta's niece to the cemetery where they had a picnic at Nesta's graveside and sang Happy Birthday.

After Nesta's death Eleanor sold 6 Hammersmith Terrace to people she trusted would look after it. That the house should be cared for appropriately was a matter of great importance to her. She had given Thatched Cottage to Virginia on the same principle. Hammersmith Terrace had outlived its purpose however so she now bought Nesta's Camden Street house. She wrote to Hugh:

> 6 Hammersmith Terrace – can't help missing it but it's OK – time was UP! I am in the midst of exchanging houses & I didn't know what I was undertaking... unbelievable quantities of money to be exchanged on both sides just cancel "New-wealth" straight out, so one is back to good old middle class![6]

Most of the Hammersmith Terrace furnishings went to the sale room but her eight Robert Austin drawings were hung around the walls of the sitting room and on the stairs at Camden Street.

Eleanor's bedroom was on the first floor overlooking the street. There was a window box and there were always flowers in the room – Eleanor's favourite flowers were anemones. Around her she kept books – an anthology with poems by Christina Rossetti given to her by Laurence on her seventeenth birthday, the Bible, works of Gurdjieff, the poetry of T.S. Eliot (who had also known Bosham), a book on Norwegian churches. Her pictures were on the walls as well as the photograph of Gurdjieff. More of her watercolours were propped up around the room as well as family pictures. A postcard-sized photograph of Robert Austin, as he must have looked when she first knew him, stood on the shelves opposite her bed.

New friends and neighbours arrived at the end of Eleanor's life – drawn to her because she was such excellent company, so interesting, such fun to talk to. Among them were Hugh

Hamrick, an artist and theatre designer, and his partner, the writer David Sedaris. Every week Hamrick brought her flowers from the Portobello Road and he showed her his own drawings for her comments. She encouraged him to work. Sometimes he read her Sedaris's stories – although by this time she was deaf and he had to raise his voice which he found hard. But she tired quickly. To his amusement one evening in 2008, after they had both agreed that the election of Barack Obama would be a good thing she told him, 'Now that we have settled the future of the world I think you can go.'

Eleanor spent as much time as possible at Bosham. It was the place which gave her the most joy in the world and in the summer she stayed for weeks on end. She wrote to Virginia after her mother Joan's death:

> I am writing in bed at 6 am on a divine Bosham early morning, sun on trees, waving grasses, ox-eye daisies & glorious wild irises around the ponds - my writing is v. skew-whiff & I hope you can read it (I have so little time of privacy).[7]

There was a stair-lift and she would descend from her bedroom waving regally to amuse guests. Often she sat for hours on end at the window or in the garden with a pair of binoculars watching the seabirds as they wheeled and curved in the wind or gathered around the tidal creeks and rivulets where sea and land met. She had hoped that the sale of 6 Hammersmith Terrace would cover all her debts and forthcoming expenditure but her care costs continued to rise and she took out a private banking loan. She spent long periods of 2008 in Bosham but she was physically able to go much less often the following year. Had she lived at Meadow House permanently she could not have relied on the constant presence of Ellen and her other carers and doctors. She would also have missed her Gurdjieff meetings so she agreed to its sale. Buyers were found who, she hoped, could be trusted to look after the house, the garden and the wild flower meadow without spoiling them. But she underestimated the psychological blow caused by the sale of her house by the sea. At the end her life it was a bitter blow. Afterwards she said she would not have returned even if it had been possible. She was growing increasingly weaker and she admitted that losing Bosham broke her heart.

Eleanor nursed her feelings for Austin for over seventy years. After Nesta's death she inquired whether she could be buried in St Nicholas's, the parish church of Chiswick where Austin lay, but the churchyard was full. The sense of what might have been continued to haunt her. She told an interviewer from a Bosham paper which published articles about local residents that the reason she had never had children was that she had been unable to marry the man she loved 'because of the conventions of the time'. But the remark seems disingenuous. When, in her most private conversations she talked about 'Bob', her eyes still welled up with tears. She directed that Robert Austin's letters to her were to be destroyed after her death, a request which was fulfilled. Eleanor outlived Sarah Sproule who died in 2006.

Eleanor had a dread of the physical processes of death and the sensations involved – she had been too close before. There was a very real fear of anything that might bring on her heart condition or any other infections. To the young she said forcefully, never get old! Yet Eleanor hung to life incredibly positively. There was no stoic resignation about dying. For all her sweetness she had a rod of steel. She wanted to live even into old age: in spite of her physical limitations, she felt – especially in the Gurdjieff work – there was still so much to discover, and to achieve. With tremendous difficulty, Ellen still managed to get her into her car and take her to the weekly meetings almost to the very end. Ellen also read to her from Gurdjieff's writings. She was only just beginning to understand him, Eleanor said. Perhaps the Gurdjieff work with all its emphasis on self-development, and of becoming aware of the mechanical automatisms that dominate our conscious and unconscious lives only sharpens that sense of having achieved far too little near the end. '[8]Her self-blame for not working changed her last years to a positive hunger for being.' A sense of 'not now, not yet' was around until remarkably late. It only began to ebb at last when the physical burdens became very great. She was sustained too by her Anglican faith.

Eleanor would sometimes say, 'This is no way to live,' or 'Let's speed it up.' One evening she told Ellen that she could not bear any more of her 'life or death' pills and refused to take them but all that happened was that she fell asleep and in the morning wanted breakfast for the first time in years.

A large party for friends and family was held on her ninety-ninth birthday. You must tell the story of my life, Eleanor said. 'Hers was a marvellous friendship,' an old friend, Pat Feltham, said of Eleanor: knowing that Eleanor thought the cello made the most beautiful music of all, as a birthday present she arranged for a cellist to come and play for her in her bedroom.

Two days later, in the early hours of the morning of March 9th 2011, Eleanor died. At the side of her grave in Marylebone Cemetery, very close to that of Nesta and their other friends, a mourner spoke the words of Christina Rossetti's, 'In the Bleak Mid-Winter', a favourite poem. And a white dove was released from its cage.

1 EEH memoir

2 'My secret is my own' *literally* 'my secret unto myself'

3 Nesta Brooking to Sarah Seymour, undated.

4 Roses from one of the flower pictures were carved as a cartouche by the artist Ross Fuller on EEH's gravestone.

5 Edmund Hudson to EEH, 17 February 1974

6 EEH to Hugh Hudson, 28 April 2008

7 EEH to Virginia Costa, 2 June 2004

8 Obituary, The Gurdjieff Society Annual Report, April 2010 – March 2011

Clean Shirt
watercolour on blue-grey paper

Institutions holding works by Erlund Hudson

UNITED KINGDOM
British Museum, London

Imperial War Museum, London

Royal Watercolour Society, London

Wellcome Library, London

Ashmolean Museum, Oxford (Royal Society of Painter-Printmakers Diploma Collection)

Brighton Museum and Art Gallery

Dudley Museum and Art Gallery

Torre Abbey, Torquay, Devon

USA
Museum of Fine Arts, Boston

Smithsonian American Art Museum, Washington DC

Yale Center for British Art, New Haven, Connecticut

CANADA
National Gallery of Canada, Ottawa

The Ball Dress
etching

Pictures exhibited by Erlund Hudson

ROYAL ACADEMY

1935

1275 Lamplight, etching
1342 The Kitchen, etching

1936

1322 The Ball Dress, etching

1937

1184 The Lantern, etching
1213 The Picture, etching

1938

1227 Attic Bedroom, etching
1233 Girl in a Library, etching

1939

962 River Wall, etching
994 Window Seat, etching
1006 Interior, etching

1940

1247 Interior, Verona, etching
1274 Italian Flower Seller, etching
1333 Wineshop, Verona, etching

1946

994 Summer Morning, charcoal
1000 The Striped Blouse, charcoal

1947

701 Woman in her Kitchen
713 Girl Reading
834 Girl Sewing

1948

744 The Pink Skirt
1151 The Cobbler and his Wife, etching

1949

1090 Fireside Study, etching	1158 Woman Sponging her Baby's Face, etching	1163 Supper-time, etching

1950

805 Spring Posy	850 Prelude to Theatricals	857 The Coiffure

1951

681 Girl with Newspaper	741 The Young Traveller, chalk and ink	976 The Sewing Room, etching

1952

1052 Dancer Resting		

1953

756 Ballet Wardrobe	772 Woman at her Toilet	1041 Dancer and Dressers, etching

1954

819 Two Dancers in a Studio		

ROYAL SOCIETY OF PAINTER-ETCHERS AND ENGRAVERS

1938

23 Girl in a Library, etching	25 Dressing Room, etching	27 Lamplight, etching
24 Attic Bedroom, etching	26 Fortune Telling, etching	28 The Picture, etching

1939

50 Interior, etching	151 Three Flower Girls, etching	
61 Window Seat, etching	152 River Wall, etching	

1940

13 Fortune Telling, etching	128 Interior, Verona, etching	232 Study, drawing
75 Summer Night, Verona, etching	144 A Wine Shop, Verona, etching	248 Study, drawing

1942

12 After the Bath, etching	239 Study, drypoint	
61 Attic Bedroom, engraving	246 Study, drypoint	

1945

107 Attic Bedroom, engraving
111 Three Flower Girls, etching
165 Study – Dressing Room Scene, engraving
174 Dressing Room, engraving
180 Interior, engraving
222 Study for a Portrait, drawing
229 Fireside Study, drawing

1946

2 Italian Flower Seller, engraving
14 Wineshop, Verona, engraving
15 Summer Night, Verona, engraving
27 The Window Seat engraving
261 Woman with a Newspaper, drawing
262 Girl Sleeping, drawing
285 Study for the Attic Bedroom, drawing
290 Study – the Travellers, drawing

1947

195 Head of an Old Woman, drawing
203 Fireside, drawing
210 Girl with a book, drawing
215 Study, Head of a Young Girl, drawing

1948

148 The Cobbler and His Wife, etching
157 The Mirror, etching
166 Fireside, etching
181 Woman Sponging her Baby's Face, etching
193 Supper-time, etching
209 Woman Brushing Her Hair, drawing
216 Young Girl at a Table, drawing
223 The Model's Rest, drawing

1950

92 Harvester Saying Grace, etching
284 Dancer's Reverie, drawing
291 Dancer holding her ankle, drawing
304 Study for Dressing Room Corner, drawing
306 Study for "The Coiffure", drawing

1951

168 The Sewing Room (no technique given)
172 Studio Corner

1953

4 Dancers' Dressing Room, etching
10 Dancer and Rocking Chair, etching
23 Dancer and Dressers, etching

SOCIETY OF ARTIST PRINTMAKERS

1938

6 Attic Bedroom, etching
31 Dressing Room, etching
35 Fortune Telling, etching
123 After the Bath, etching

1939

75 Lumber Room, etching
79 Fortune Telling, etching
83 Window Seat, etching
86 Attic Bedroom, etching
173 The Picture, etching

1940

67 Interior, etching
71 Italian Flower Seller, etching
106 Wineshop, Verona, etching

ROYAL WATERCOLOUR SOCIETY

Spring 1939

149 Woman Dressing
158 Restaurant
167 Artist

Autumn 1939

167 Girl Sewing
178 Under the Awnings
180 Channel Crossing

Spring 1940

56 Morning
72 Lavandaria
86 The Artist
89 The Audition

Spring 1942

1 Girl with Dancing Shoes
68 Restaurant Scene
72 Girl Reading

Spring 1944

73 Girl Reading
77 Girl in a Green Smock
188 Canteen Kitchen

Spring 1946

51 Woman in Her Kitchen
78 Woman in a Studio
164 The Little Sewing Machine

Autumn 1946

33 Washing Day	53 Day-Dream	206 After Tea
38 The New Book	193 The Pink Shirt	

Spring 1947

54 Afternoon Rest	73 Woman Sewing	80 Reverie

Autumn 1947

14 The Sewing Room	28 The Dressmaker	32 Evening

Spring 1948

52 Woman with a Big Book	82 Girl Ironing	153 Woman Cutting Out

Autumn 1948

161 Girl Darning		

Autumn 1949

64 Spring Posy	142 The Coiffure	
129 Old Lady's Airing	205 Prelude to Theatricals	

Spring 1950

12 The New Dress	32 The Letter	

Autumn 1950

67 Le Petit Tombeau	109 Girl on a Couch	130 Bretenoux

Spring 1951

84 Woman at her Toilet	88 The Yellow Skirt	222 Tired Girl

Autumn 1951

15 Ballet Wardrobe	29 Dancer Resting	

Spring 1952

49 Girl Making Ballet Skirts		

Autumn 1953

1 Margarita – Third Position

44 Selena Resting

Spring 1954

5 Daydream

15 Thalia Resting

Autumn 1954

160 Dancers in a Studio

Spring 1956

129 Summer Peace

Spring 1957

40 Meditation on Spring

Spring 1999

3 Lady at Her Toilet

Spring 2000

33 The Coiffure

Autumn 2000

110 Thalia Resting

Spring 2001

29 Girl With a Newspaper

Spring 2002

36 Contemplation (c 1958)

Sources

The primary sources for this book have been the Hudson family archives, mainly those belonging to the Executors of the state of Paige Hudson, and also various papers of individual family members. In addition I have used correspondence and diaries and other papers belonging to Eleanor herself including an autobiographical memoir she wrote a few years before her death. I am grateful to Sarah Seymour for making available correspondence from Eleanor and from Nesta Brooking; to Ian Whiteman for a memoir by his aunt Nesta Brooking; and to Roland Goslett for the transcript of an interview he made with Eleanor. Interviews Eleanor recorded with her niece Virginia Da Costa and with the Imperial War Museum were also invaluable. I also made use of the archives of the Royal Watercolour Society and the Royal Society of Painter-Printmakers at Bankside Gallery as well as the correspondence of Molly Bernhard-Smith at the City of Wesminster Archives Centre.

Unfortunately very little has been published about Eleanor Hudson but the following were useful sources of additional information:

Peter Brook, *Threads of Time, A Memoir,* 1998

Simon Fenwick, *The Enchanted River, A History of the Royal Watercolour Society,* 2004

Arnold Haskell, Mark Bonham Carter and Michael Wood, *Gala Performance, A Record of the Sadler's Wells Ballet over Twenty-Five Years,* 1955

Howard Hodgkin, 'How to Be an Artist', *Burlington Magazine,* September 1982

Howard Hodgkin, Tate Publishing, 2006

J. Johnson and A. Greutzner, *The Dictionary of British Artists 1880 - 1940*

Jacob Needleman, *Introduction to the Gurdjieff Work,* 2009

Kathleen Palmer, *Women War Artists,* 2011

Robert Austin, Exhibition of Etchings, Engravings, and Drawings, Ashmolean Museum, Oxford, February – March 1940

The Gurdjieff Society Annual Report, April 2010 – March 2011

Untitled (portrait of woman seen at Earls Court Underground)
graphite

Picture credits

p9, p10, p12, p28 Alan Hudson

p13, p20 Exors. of Paige Hudson

p18 Virginia Da Costa née Hudson

p25, p34, p35, p37, p43, p44, p75, p106 Exors. of Eleanor Hudson

p26, p27, p31, p33, p41, p43, p47, p49, p51, p57, p59, p65, p69, p71, p114 Royal Watercolour Society

p55 Hugh Hamrick

p67, p88 Myrth Russell née Hudson

p73 Collection of Dudley Museum and Art Gallery, Dudley MBC

p76 Prue Seward

p77 Courtesy of Pocock's the Artmonger

p79 Ian Whiteman

p83, p93, p98 Sarah Seymour

p84 Andreas Basler

p87 Kim Mendez

p97 Hugh Hudson

p100 Ellen Garcia

p104 Courtesy of Sim Fine Art